Observer's Books

NATURAL HISTORY
Birds · Birds' Eggs · Wild Animals · Zoo Animals · Farm
Animals · Freshwater Fishes · Sea Fishes · Tropical
Fishes · Butterflies · Larger Moths · Insects and Spiders
Pond Life · Sea and Seashore · Sea-shells · Dogs · Horses
and Ponies · Cats · Pets · Trees · Wild Flowers · Grasses
Mushrooms · Lichens · Cacti · Garden Flowers
Flowering Shrubs · House Plants · Vegetables · Geology
Weather · Astronomy · Fossils

SPORT
Association Football · Cricket · Golf · Coarse Fishing
Fly Fishing · Show Jumping · Motor Sport

TRANSPORT
Automobiles · Aircraft · Commercial Vehicles
Motorcycles · Steam Locomotives · Ships · Small Craft
Manned Spaceflight · Unmanned Spaceflight

ARCHITECTURE
Architecture · Churches · Cathedrals

COLLECTING
Awards and Medals · Coins · Postage Stamps · Glass
Pottery and Porcelain · Firearms

ARTS AND CRAFTS
Music · Painting · Modern Art · Sculpture · Furniture
Sewing

HISTORY AND GENERAL INTEREST
Ancient Britain · Flags · Heraldry · European Costume

TRAVEL
London · Tourist Atlas GB · Cotswolds · Lake District

The Observer's Book of

AUTOMOBILES

Compiled by the
OLYSLAGER ORGANISATION

Edited by
DAVID VOLLER
and
CAROL ALEXANDER

FREDERICK WARNE

LONDON

First Edition 1955
Twenty-first Edition 1978

NOTE

The specifications contained in this book were collated on the basis of material available to the compilers up to the end of October 1977. All information is subject to change and/or cancellation during the course of the model year. Although every effort has been made to ensure correctness in compiling this book, responsibility for inaccuracies and omissions cannot be accepted by the compilers and publishers.

LIBRARY OF CONGRESS CATALOG
CARD NO. 62–9807

ISBN 0 7232 1585 5
Printed in Great Britain by
William Clowes & Sons Limited
London, Beccles and Colchester

FOREWORD

Now in its 21st edition, the Observer's Book of Automobiles has long since come of age and indeed has regularly turned the key to reveal the changing face of the motor car over the last quarter of a century.

This latest edition includes many new and modified models, including Chrysler's new Sunbeam which takes over the Company's small car spot vacated by the quiet passing of the Imp range in 1976, the BMW 733, Ford Granada Ghia, Mercedes Benz 280 Coupe and Rover 2300/2600 range. Unquestionably the most bizarre newcomer, however, is the Panther 6, complete with six wheels, twin turbo-charged 8.2 litre V-8 engine, automatic fire extinguishing system and push-button telephone.

As a complete break with tradition the model featured on the dust jacket of this latest edition is not a normal production car but an example of what the creators of fantasy in the world of the cinema can achieve with a sleek production sports model.

One notable absentee from this book is the immortal Volkswagen Beetle, which has appeared in every previous edition but has finally been discontinued after a truly remarkable production run stretching back to the second World War.

As in previous years the co-operation and encouragement of the various manufacturers and concessionaires has been invaluable and their efforts are greatly appreciated.

KEY TO DATA

1. Manufacturer and Country of Origin. The growth of integrated production—national and international—has brought a trend to use parent company names and we have attempted to reflect manufacturers' own attitudes in this respect. Chrysler and Leyland models, for example, are listed under these headings instead of Hillman or Triumph. There will no doubt be noticeable changes in this respect in future Observer's books.

2. Model Designation. Designations vary from market to market. The Cortina of the UK is the Taunus of Germany; the Hunter of UK is the Paykan (Arrow) of Iran; the Wartburg 353 of East Germany is the Knight of the UK.

3. Engine Size. Engine size is quoted in cubic centimetres for the standard engine of the model shown. Alternative engines are quoted under 'Notes'.

4. Chassis. Most current production cars have a 'monocoque' or unitary body-cum-chassis construction which implies that the body and the frame members are welded together to form one unit. Many of the heavier cars, especially in the USA still have a separate chassis frame or a combination of the two. Some for example, have a boxed 'perimeter' frame extending to the back of the passenger compartment and integral construction at the rear. Others have a 'space frame' or sub-frames for the mounting of the engine and suspension units.

5. Engine. Engine location, number and layout of cylinders are given. Valve actuation is either by means of a camshaft and push rods (ohv) or by a direct-acting overhead camshaft (ohc). Rotary and two-stroke engines do not have valves.

Bore (cylinder diameter) and stroke (piston travel) are quoted in millimetres. To convert to inches multiply by 0.03937.

Output is quoted in bhp (brake horse power); the German DIN standard is quoted where possible. In some instances the American SAE has to be given in the absence of a DIN figure. To convert to Kilowatts (kW) multiply by 0.746.

Torque (twisting effort by the engine) is quoted in kgf.m. (kilograms force metres) and lbf.ft (pounds force feet). Again, DIN figures are used when available.

6. Carburettor. 'Single' means one carburettor even though it may be one, two- or four-barrelled. Many American cars have two- or four-barrel options. Despite one or two switches away from fuel-injection equipment there is still an increase in its application. Where a fuel-injection system is used instead of the carburettor the feature is highlighted under 'Notes'.

7. Clutch. Most cars with manual transmission are now fitted with a single dry plate (sdp) clutch, often with a diaphragm-type release spring. Actuation of the clutch (transmission of movement from pedal to clutch release mechanism) is either hydraulic and basically similar to the hydraulic brake system or mechanical by means of a rod or cable. Cars with semi- or fully-automatic transmission usually have a torque converter but some have a fluid coupling, e.g. Bentley, Mercedes-Benz, Rolls-Royce.

8. Transmission. '3F1R' indicates three forward speeds, one reverse. A four-speed unit is indicated as '4F1R'. Manual gearboxes are usually controlled by a floor-mounted lever but in some instances a steering column-mounted lever is optional or standard. If all forward gears are fitted with synchromesh this is indicated by 'a/s'. Many US car manufacturers offer either three- or four-speed gearboxes sometimes with a choice of ratios. On certain cars top gear is overdrive (meaning a lower ratio than the customary 1 : 1 'direct drive'); on some others there is a separate overdrive unit.

Automatic transmission. In the USA about 80 per cent of new cars are delivered with automatic transmission, which is usually an optional extra but which on certain cars comes as standard equipment. On some models there is a choice of more than one type. In other countries the automatic is rapidly gaining ground especially on medium and top-line models. For small cars the relatively high extra cost still proves a considerable barrier to 'two pedal motoring'. A notable exception is the 'Variomatic' automatic transmission (by far the simplest and cheapest in the world) originally fitted on DAF models and since the integration with Volvo now used on the smallest Volvo models. Semi-automatics are less in evidence than in years gone by, but some European cars such as NSU Ro80, Porsche and VW offer a combination of a torque converter with a conventional gearbox. On such cars the need for gear shifting is minimized due to the torque converter. When shifting up or down is required this is done by simply moving the lever, which action automatically disconnects the drive by means of an electric contact built into the gear lever knob.

9. Final Drive. Refers to driven wheels (i.e. front, rear or all). All-wheel drive models have a separate gearbox to allow one axle to be engaged only when necessary).

10. Brakes. The growing use of disc brakes and servo-assistance will be apparent to readers of earlier Observer books. Disc brakes on front and rear are featured on many performance and top-line models. Disc brakes have a much greater resistance to fade than drum brakes but do not require greater pedal pressure if there is no servo assistance.

11.   Steering. Use of rack and pinion or recirculating ball is now almost universal, the former preferred by Europe and the latter by North America. Power-assistance is offered on bigger and top-line models.

12.   Suspension. Front wheels are independently sprung with only very few exceptions. Springs used are usually of the coil or torsion bar type, the former either with wishbones of unequal length or combined with shock absorbers, forming a 'suspension strut'. Some cars have transversal leaf springs, other notable exceptions to usual practice being some British Leyland models whch employ the 'Hydrolastic' rubber-and-fluid system, interconnecting the front and rear suspension at each side and the larger Citroens whch feature a sophisticated self-levelling hydro-pneumatic system.

Most American and Japanese manufacturers in the main stick to the conventional 'live' rear axle layout whereby the car is suspended by means of either semi-elliptical single- or multi-leaf or coil springs. In Europe the tendency is very much towards an independent rear suspension system of various configurations. Another tendency on top-line models is the use of self-levelling devices.

13.   Tyres. Sizes shown are the standard fitment for the model shown; model variations may have different tyres. Radial ply tyres are now predominant although cross-ply and bias belted are still to be found, the latter especially in North America. Tyre coding presents a bewildering variety; as a rule tyre width is quoted (5.20, 6.00 in inches, 155, 185 etc., in mm) as in wheel rim (13, 15 etc. in inches; 330, 380 etc. in mm). Most tyres are now tubeless.

14. Dimensions. Overall dimensions for the illustrated model are quoted.

15. Wheelbase. Distance between front and rear wheel centres.

16. Weight. The unladen weight quoted is normally the manufacturer's kerb weight. The variety of ways that kerb weight are calculated means figures must be taken as a rough guide to the vehicle's weight without passengers, driver and luggage.

17. Capacities. Metric measurements are given followed by imperial measurements in brackets. To convert from Imperial to US gallons or pints multiply by 1.2. Some engines are air cooled and in such cases no cooling system capacity is given. Fuel tank capacities include any reserve tank where fitted.

18. Notes. This heading gives general information not quoted in the specification such as engine options, unusual features, introduction dates, luxury equipment and other models available. Specification changes from previous years' models are also given.

Reference is made to maximum speeds, fuel consumption and acceleration. These figures are important but tend to be academic as test conditions, specifications and driving technique all play their part.

INTERNATIONAL REGISTRATION LETTERS

These consist of one, two or three letters of the same size, usually in black, set on a white oval background. They indicate the country of origin as set out below, and are displayed by cars which are being driven in foreign countries.

They have also been used throughout this book to indicate countries of manufacture.

Not all countries subscribe to this system of identification, however. For example, a plate bearing the letters TT (Titre Temporaire) shows that the owner has temporarily registered in France, though he may have come from another country originally. The letters following TT indicate the particular district of France where the registration was taken out.

Those plates with prefixes from QA to QS are issued by the R.A.C. or the A.A. in this country to vehicles temporarily imported from abroad. Numbers prefaced by EE indicate a first temporary registration for touring from Italy.

Cars used by High Commissioners in this country carry small plates bearing the letters HC, and those used by Foreign Embassies and Legations have a plate with the letters CD in addition to their registration plates.

In the countries marked with an asterisk the rule of the road is Drive on the Left; in other countries it is Drive on the Right.

A (AT)	Austria	GBA	Alderney*	
ADN (YD)	Democratic Yemen (formerly Aden)*	GBG	Guernsey*	Channel Islands
		GBJ	Jersey*	
AFG (AF)	Afghanistan	GBM	Isle of Man	
AL	Albania	GBZ (GI)	Gibraltar	
AND (AD)	Andorra	GCA (GT)	Guatemala	
AUS (AU)	Australia*	GH	Ghana	
B (BE)	Belgium	GR	Greece	
BDS (BB)	Barbados*	GUY (GY)	Guyana* (formerly British Guiana)	
BG	Bulgaria			
BH (BZ)	Belize (formerly British Honduras)	H (HU)	Hungary	
		HK	Hong Kong*	
BR	Brazil	HKJ (JO)	Jordan	
BRN (BH)	Bahrain	I (IT)	Italy	
BRU (BN)	Brunei*	IL	Israel	
BS	Bahamas*	IND (IN)	India*	
BUR (BU)	Burma	IR	Iran	
C (CU)	Cuba	IRL (IE)	Ireland*	
CDN (CA)	Canada	IRQ (IQ)	Iraq	
CH	Switzerland	IS	Iceland	
CI	Ivory Coast	J (JP)	Japan*	
CL (LK)	Sri Lanka (formerly Ceylon)*	JA (JM)	Jamaica*	
		K (KH)	Khmer Republic (formerly Cambodia)	
CO	Colombia			
CR	Costa Rica	KWT (KW)	Kuwait	
CS	Czechoslovakia	L (LU)	Luxembourg	
CY	Cyprus*	LAO (LA)	Laos	
D (DE)	German Federal Republic	LAR (LY)	Libya	
DDR (DD)	German Democratic Republic	LB (LR)	Liberia	
		LS	Lesotho (formerly Basutoland)*	
DK	Denmark			
DOM (DG)	Dominican Republic	M (MT)	Malta*	
DY	Dahomey	MA	Morocco	
DZ	Algeria	MAL (MY)	Malaysia*	
E (ES)	Spain (including African localities and provinces)	MC	Monaco	
		MEX (MX)	Mexico	
		MB (MU)	Mauritius*	
EAK (KE)	Kenya*	MW	Malawi*	
EAT (TZ)	Tanzania (formerly Tanganika)	N (NO)	Norway	
		NA (AN)	Netherlands Antilles	
EAU (UG)	Uganda*	NIC (NI)	Nicaragua	
EAZ (TZ)	Tanzania (formerly Zanzibar)*	NL	Netherlands	
		NZ	New Zealand*	
EC	Ecuador	P (PT)	Portugal	
ET (EG)	Arab Republic of Egypt	P (AO)	Angola	
F (FR)	France (including overseas departments and territories)	P (CV)	Cape Verde Islands	
		P (MZ)	Mozambique*	
		P (GN)	Guinea	
FJI (FJ)	Fiji*	P (TP)	Timor	
FL (LI)	Liechtenstein	P (ST)	São Tomé and Principe	
GB	United Kingdom of Great Britain and Northern Ireland*	PA	Panama	
		PAK (PK)	Pakistan*	
		PE	Peru	
		PL	Poland	

13

PY	Paraguay	SU	Union of Soviet Socialist Republics
R (RO)	Romania		
RA (AR)	Argentina	SWA	South West Africa*
RB (RW)	Botswana (formerly Bechuanaland)*	SY (SC)	Seychelles*
		SYR (SY)	Syria
RC (TW)	Taiwan (Formosa)	T (TH)	Thailand*
RCA (CF)	Central African Republic	TG	Togo
RCB (CG)	Congo	TN	Tunisia
RCH (CL)	Chile	TR	Turkey
RH (HT)	Haiti	TT	Trinidad and Tobago*
RI (ID)	Indonesia*	U (UY)	Uruguay
RIM (MR)	Mauritania	USA (US)	United States of America
RL (LB)	Lebanon	V (VA)	Holy See (Vatican City)
RM (MG)	Malagasy Republic (formerly Madagascar)	VN (VD)	Vietnam (Republic of)
		WAG (GM)	Gambia
RMM (ML)	Mali	WAL (SL)	Sierra Leone
ROK (KP)	Korea (Republic of)	WAN (NG)	Nigeria
RP (PH)	Philippines	WD (DM)	Dominica*
RSM (SM)	San Marino	WG (GD)	Granada*
RSR (RH)	Rhodesia (formerly Southern Rhodesia)*	WL (LC)	St Lucia*
		WS	Western Samoa*
RU (BI)	Burundi	WV (VC)	St Vincent (Windward Islands)*
RWA (RW)	Rwanda		
S (SE)	Sweden	YU	Yugoslavia
SD (SZ)	Swaziland*	YV (VE)	Venezuela
SF (FI)	Finland	Z	Zambia
SGP (SG)	Singapore*	ZA	South Africa*
SME (SR)	Surinam (Dutch Guiana)*	ZR (ZM)	Zaire (formerly Congo Kinshasha)
SN	Senegal		

WD (DM), WG (GD), WL (LC) } Windward Islands

AC (GB)

ME 3000

2993cc

Chassis: platform frame.
Engine: centre-mounted, six-cylinder, V-configuration, ohv, water-cooled, bore 93.7mm, stroke 72.4mm, output 140 bhp at 5500 rev/min, torque 24 kgf.m (173 lbf.ft) at 3000 rev/min, compression ratio: 9:1.
Carburettor: Weber, single.
Clutch: diaphragm, sdp.
Transmission: 5F1R, manual a/s.
Final Drive: rear wheels.
Brakes: disc front and rear, servo-assistance optional.
Steering: rack and pinion.
Suspension: independent coil springs front and rear.
Tyres: 205/60 14.
Dimensions, length: 3988mm (13ft 1in); width: 1651mm (5ft 5in); height: 1143mm (3ft 9in); wheelbase: 2300mm (7ft 6.5in); weight-unladen: 885 kg (1950 lb).
Capacities, engine sump: 6.3 litres (11 Imp. pints); fuel tank: 55 litres (14 Imp. gal); cooling system: 11.4 litres (20 Imp. pints).

   Notes: Introduced 1973. Powered by a Ford 3-litre V-6 engine set transversely in the car behind the cockpit and connected to an AC designed gearbox.

ALFA ROMEO (I)

ALFASUD 1300 Ti

1286cc

Chassis: unitary construction.
Engine: front-mounted, four-horizontally opposed cylinders, ohc, water-cooled, bore 80mm, stroke 59mm, output 76 bhp at 6000 rev/min, torque 10.5 kgf.m (76 lbf.ft) at 3500 rev/min, compression ratio: 9:1.
Carburettor: Weber, single.
Clutch: diaphragm, sdp.
Transmission: 5F1R, manual a/s.
Final Drive: front wheels.
Brakes: disc front and rear, servo-assisted.
Steering: rack and pinion.
Suspension: independent coil springs front, coil spring rear.
Tyres: 165/70SR 13.
Dimensions: length: 3930mm (12ft 10.5in); width: 1590mm (5ft 2.25in); height: 1370mm (4ft 6in); wheelbase: 2450mm (8ft 0.5in); weight-unladen: 810 kg (1782 lb).
Capacities: engine sump: 4 litres (7 Imp. pints); fuel tank: 50 litres (11 Imp. gal); cooling system: 7 litres (12 Imp. pints).
   Notes: Introduced 1974. Also available are the 5 M and 1200 Ti. Top speed 160 km/h (100 mph).

ALFA ROMEO (I)

ALFETTA 2000

1962cc

Chassis: unitary construction.
Engine: front-mounted, four-cylinder, in-line, ohc, water-cooled, bore 84mm, stroke 88.5mm, output 125 bhp at 5300 rev/min, torque 17.9 kgf.m (13 lbf.ft) at 4000 rev/min, compression ratio: 9.0:1.
Carburettor: Solex twin.
Clutch: diaphragm, sdp.
Transmission: 5F1R, manual a/s.
Final Drive: rear wheels.
Brakes: disc front and rear, servo-assisted.
Steering: rack and pinion.
Suspension: independent torsion bars front, coil springs rear.
Tyres: 165 HR 14.
Dimensions, length: 4385mm (14ft 3in); width: 1640mm (5ft 4in); height: 1430mm (4ft 8in); wheelbase: 2510mm (8ft 3in); weight-unladen: 1140 kg (2514 lb).
Capacities, engine sump: 7.05 litres (12.5 Imp. pints); fuel tank: 49 litres (10.75 Imp. gal); cooling system: 8 litres (14 Imp. pints).
   Notes: Introduced in the UK late 1977. Specification includes De Dion rear axle and rear mounted clutch/gearbox/hypoid drive. Maximum speed is 185 km/h (117 mph).

AMERICAN MOTORS (USA)

GREMLIN

1984cc

Chassis: unitary construction.
Engine: front-mounted, four-cylinder, in-line, ohv, water-cooled, bore 86.5mm, stroke 84.4mm, output 81 bhp at 5000 rev/min, torque 14.5 kgf.m (104.8 lbf.ft).
Carburettor: Carter, single.
Clutch sdp.
Transmission: 4F1R, manual, a/s.
Final Drive: rear wheels.
Brakes: disc front, drum rear, servo-assistance optional.
Steering: recirculating ball.
Suspension: independent coil spring front, leaf spring rear.
Tyres: DR 78 14.
Dimensions: length: 4216mm (13ft 10in); width: 1791mm (5ft 10.5in); height: 1308mm (4ft 3.5in); wheelbase: 2440mm (8ft 0in).
Capacities: engine sump: 4.3 litres (7½ Imp. pints); fuel tank: 57 litres (12½ Imp. gal); cooling system: 6.5 litres (11½ Imp. pints).
   Notes: Available as basic 6-cyl. model and as custom model with either 2-litre 4-cyl. or 6-cyl. engine. Model shown has the optional 'X' sports pack fitted. Latest Gremlin models have a number of refinements, primarily to the interior fittings.

AMERICAN MOTORS (USA)

PACER

3802cc

Chassis: unitary construction.
Engine: front-mounted, six-cylinder, in-line, ohv, water-cooled, bore 95.2mm, stroke 88.9mm, output 90 bhp at 3050 rev/min, torque 23 kgf.m (163 lbf.ft) at 2200 rev/min, compression ratio 8.0:1.
Carburettor: Carter, single.
Clutch: sdp.
Transmission: 3F1R, manual a/s.
Final Drive: rear wheels.
Brakes: disc front, drum rear, servo-assistance optional.
Steering: Rack and pinion, power-assistance optional.
Suspension: independent coil spring front, leaf spring rear.
Tyres: D78 14.
Dimensions: length: 4320mm (14ft 2in); width: 1960mm (6ft 5in); height: 1340mm (4ft 4.75in); wheelbase: 2540mm (8ft 4in); weight: 1470 kg (3241 lb).
Capacities: engine sump: 4.7 litres (8¼ Imp. pints); fuel tank: 83.2 litres (18¼ Imp. gal); cooling system: 13.2 litres (23¼ Imp. pints).
   Note: Hatchback (shown) and 2-door wagon versions available. Latest models have modified front end and bonnet, revised wheel trims, tyres and internal fittings. Alternative 6-cyl. 258 CID and V-8 304 CID engines and various gearboxes optionally available.

AMERICAN MOTORS (USA)

CONCORD   3802cc

Chassis: unitary construction.
Engine: front-mounted, six-cylinder, in-line, ohv, water-cooled, bore 95.2mm, stroke 88.9mm, output 90 bhp at 3050 rev/min, torque 23 kgf.m (163 lbf.ft) at 2200 rev/min, compression ratio 8.0:1.
Carburettor: Carter, single.
Clutch: sdp.
Transmission: 3F1R, manual a/s.
Final Drive: rear wheels.
Brakes: disc front, drum rear, servo-assistance optional.
Steering: recirculating ball, power-assistance optional.
Suspension: independent coil spring front, leaf spring rear.
Tyres: C78 x 14.
Dimensions: length: 4674mm (15ft 4in); width: 1803mm (5ft 11in); height: 1321mm (4ft 4in); wheelbase: 2743mm (9ft 0in).
Capacities: engine sump: 4.7 litres (8¼ Imp. pints); fuel tank: 83 litres (22 US gal); cooling system: 13.2 litres (23¼ Imp. pints).
   Notes: Introduced 1977. New luxury compact model available in four body styles: hatchback (shown) 2- and 4-door sedans and station wagon. Rectangular headlamps and bezels make it easily distinguishable from other current American Motors models. Various optional engines and gearboxes available.

AMERICAN MOTORS (USA)

MATADOR

4229cc

Chassis: unitary construction.
Engine: front-mounted, six-cylinder, in-line, ohv, water-cooled, bore 95mm, stroke 99mm, output 95 bhp at 3050 rev/min, torque 24.7 kgf.m (179 lbf.ft) at 2100 rev/min, compression ratio 8:1.
Carburettor: Carter, single.
Clutch: sdp.
Transmission: 3F1R, manual, a/s.
Final Drive: rear wheels.
Brakes: disc front, drum rear, servo-assisted.
Steering: recirculating ball.
Suspension: independent coil spring front, coil spring rear.
Tyres: E78 x 14.
Dimensions, length: 5490mm (18ft 0in); width: 1920mm (6ft 3.75in); height: 1390mm (4ft 6.75in); wheelbase: 3000mm (9ft 10in); weight-unladen: 1673 kg (3864 lb).
Capacities, engine sump: 4.8 litres (8.5 Imp. pints); fuel tank: 93 litres (22 Imp. gal); cooling system: 10 litres (17.5 imp. pints).
  Notes: Available as 2-door coupé, 4-door sedan and 4-door station wagon. Version shown is the 4-door sedan fitted with the Barcelona option luxury package which was previously available only on the coupé. Various engine and gearbox combinations optionally available.

ASTON MARTIN (GB)

LAGONDA

5340cc

Chassis: platform frame.
Engine: front-mounted, eight-cylinder, V-configuration, ohc, water-cooled, bore 100mm, stroke 85mm.
Carburettor: Weber, four.
Transmission: 3F1R, automatic.
Final Drive: rear wheels.
Brakes: disc front and rear, servo-assisted.
Steering: rack and pinion.
Suspension: independent coil spring front, coil spring rear.
Tyres: GR 70VR 15.
Dimensions: length: 5283mm (17ft 4in); width: 1816mm (5ft 11.5in); height: 1302mm (4ft 3.25in); wheelbase: 2915mm (9ft 6.75in); weight - unladen 1727 kg (3800 lb).
Capacities: engine sump: 11.3 litres (20 Imp pints); fuel tank: 128 litres (28 Imp gal); cooling system: 18.1 litres (32 Imp pints).
   Notes: Introduced October 1976; hailed as the 'space age car'. Features touch sensitive switches (including for gear change), electronically controlled instruments with graphic digital read-offs calculated by a mini-processor. The speedometer can be changed from mph to km/h by the touch of a switch; average speed and fuel consumption for a journey can also be shown. Mechanical features include power-operated luxury seats, self-levelling rear suspension, de Dion rear axle and air-conditioning.

ASTON MARTIN (GB)

VANTAGE

5340cc

Chassis: platform frame.
Engine: front-mounted, eight-cylinder, V-configuration, ohc, water-cooled, bore 100mm, stroke 85mm.
Carburettor: Weber, four.
Clutch: diaphragm, sdp.
Transmission: 5F1R, manual, a/s.
Final Drive: rear wheels.
Brakes: discs front and rear, power-assisted.
Steering: rack and pinion, power-assisted.
Suspension: independent coil spring front, coil springs rear.
Tyres: 255 60 15 VR.
Dimensions: length: 4667mm (15ft 3.75in); width: 1829mm (6ft 0in); height: 1327mm (4ft 4$\frac{1}{4}$in); wheelbase: 2610mm (8ft 6$\frac{3}{4}$in).
Capacities: engine sump: 10.2 litres (18 Imp. pints); fuel tank: 114 litres (25 Imp. gal); cooling system: 18 litres (31.5 Imp. pints).
  Notes: Claimed to be the world's fastest accelerating current production car with acceleration to 60 mph (96 km/h) in 5.4 seconds and to 100 mph (160 km/h) in 12.9 seconds. Maximum speed is around 170 mph (274 km/h). Front air dam, revised grille, bonnet bulge cowl and rear spoiler distinguish, externally, the Vantage from the Aston Martin V8.

AUDI (D)

Chassis: unitary construction.
Engine: front-mounted, four-cylinder, in-line, ohc, water-cooled, bore 79.5mm, stroke 80mm, output 75 bhp at 5600 rev/min, torque 11.6 kgf.m (84 lbf.ft) at 3200 rev/min, compression ratio: 9.5:1.
Carburettor: Solex, single.
Clutch: diaphragm, sdp.
Transmission: 4F1R, manual a/s, 3F1R automatic optional.
Final Drive: front wheels.
Brakes: disc front, drum rear, servo-assisted.
Steering: rack and pinion.
Suspension: independent coil spring front, coil spring rear.
Tyres: 155SR 13.
Dimensions, length: 4204mm (13ft 9.5in); width: 1600mm (5ft 3in); height: 1360mm (4ft 5.5in); wheelbase: 2470mm (8ft 1.2in); weight-unladen: 855 kg (1885 lb).
Capacities, engine sump: 4 litres (7 Imp. pints); fuel tank: 45 litres (10 Imp. gall); cooling system: 8 litres (14 Imp. pints).
   Notes: Introduced 1972. Restyled model of 1977 continues unchanged. Other models are 80 GLS, LS and Estate car. The 80 GTE (fitted with fuel injection equipment) is available on certain markets.

AUDI (D)

100 LS   **1984cc**

Chassis: unitary construction.
Engine: front-mounted, four-cylinder, in-line, ohc, water-cooled, bore 86.5mm, stroke 84.4mm, output 115 bhp at 5500 rev/min, torque 16.8 kgf.m (122 lbf.ft) at 3500 rev/min, compression ratio: 9.3:1.
Carburettor: Solex, single.
Clutch: sdp.
Transmission: 4F1R, manual a/s, 3F1R automatic optional.
Final Drive: front wheels.
Brakes: disc front, drum rear, servo-assisted.
Steering: rack and pinion.
Suspension: independent coil springs front, coil springs rear.
Tyres: 165SR 14.
Dimensions, length: 4700mm (15ft 5in); width: 1780mm (5ft 10in); height: 1397mm (4ft 7in); wheelbase: 2680mm (8ft 9.5in); weight-unladen: 1150 kg (2535 lb).
Capacities, engine sump: 4 litres (7 Imp. pints); fuel tank: 60 litres (13.2 Imp. gal); cooling system: 8 litres (14 Imp. pints).
  Notes: Introduced 1968 (restyled version 1976). Powered by the Porsche 924 engine. Also available in certain markets is a five-cylinder petrol engine with fuel-injection and developing 136 bhp; a four-cylinder 116 bhp engine is also available in certain markets. A more luxurious GLS model is also available.

BENTLEY (GB)

T2　　　　　　　　　　　　　　　　　　**6750cc**

Chassis: unitary construction.
Engine: front-mounted, eight-cylinder, V-configuration, ohv, water-cooled, bore 104mm, stroke 99mm, output not disclosed, torque not disclosed, compression ratio 8:1.
Carburettor: SU, twin.
Clutch: not disclosed.
Transmission: 3F1R automatic.
Final Drive: rear wheels.
Brakes: disc front and rear, power-assisted.
Steering: rank and pinion, power-assisted.
Suspension: independent coil springs front and rear.
Tyres: HR70 HR 15.
Dimensions, length: 5200mm (17ft 0.5in); width: 1800mm (5ft 11 in); height: 1520mm (4ft 11.75in); wheelbase: 3050mm (10ft 0in); weight: unladen 2235 kg (4930 lb).
Capacities, engine sump: 8 litres (14.5 Imp pints); fuel tank: 107 litres (23.5 Imp. gal); cooling system: 16 litres (28.5 Imp. pints).
　Notes: Four-door luxury Saloon. Similar specifications to Rolls-Royce Silver Shadow II. Latest '2' version introduced early in 1977 has numerous modifications including new steering gear, revised suspension, re-designed fascia and the worlds first fully automatic two-level air conditioning system. Externally distinguishable by the front air dam and new wrap-around bumpers. Max. speed 193 km/h (120 mph) approximately.

BMW (D)

1573cc

Chassis: unitary construction.
Engine: front-mounted, four-cylinder, in-line, ohc, water-cooled, bore 84mm, stroke 71mm, output 90 bhp at 6000 rev/min, torque 12.4 kgf.m. (90 lbf.ft) at 4000 rev/min, compression ratio: 8.3:1.
Carburettor: Solex, single.
Clutch: sdp.
Transmission: 4F1R, manual a/s.
Final Drive: rear wheels.
Brakes: disc front, drum rear, servo-assisted.
Steering: rack and pinion.
Suspension: independent coil springs front and rear.
Tyres: 165SR 13.
Dimensions, length: 4380mm (14ft 3.5in); width: 1617mm (5ft 3.5in); height: 1592mm (4ft 6.25in); wheelbase: 2565mm (8ft 5in); weight-unladen: 1010 kg (2227 lb).
Capacities, engine sump: 4 litres (7 Imp. pints); fuel tank: 50 litres (11 Imp. gal); cooling system: 7 litres (12.25 Imp. pints).
   Notes: Introduced 1975. Smallest model in the '3 series' range which replaced the famous 2002 series in production since 1966. The new range features improved engines, better steering and handling and increased interior space and luxury.

BMW (D)

Chassis: unitary construction.
Engine: front-mounted, six-cylinder, in-line, ohc, water-cooled, bore 80mm, stroke 66mm, output 122 bhp at 6000 rev/min, torque 16.3 kgf.m. (160 lbf.ft) at 4000 rev/min, compression ratio: 9.2:1.
Carburettor: Solex, single.
Clutch: sdp.
Transmission: 4F1R, manual, a/s.
Final Drive: rear wheels.
Brakes: disc front, drum rear, servo-assisted.
Steering: rack and pinion.
Suspension: independent coil springs front and rear.
Tyres: 185/70HR 13.
Dimensions, length: 4355mm (14ft 2in); width: 1617mm (5ft 3.5in); height: 1380mm (4ft 6in); wheelbase: 2565mm (8ft 5in); weight unladen: 1115 kg (2459 lb).
Capacities, engine sump: 4.3 litres (7.5 Imp. pints); fuel tank: 58 litres (12.8 Imp. gal); cooling system: 7.1 litres (12.25 Imp. pints).
   Notes: Introduced 1975. One of the '3 series' range. Latest version fitted with a new 2-litre, 6-cylinder engine, revised rear axle ratio, wider tyres and modified suspension. Also available is the 323 i which is powered by a new 2.3 litr, 143 bhp engine with fuel injection, and the 316 (see preceding entry).

BMW (D)

Chassis: unitary construction.
Engine: front-mounted, six-cylinder, in-line, ohc, water-cooled, bore 80mm, stroke 66mm, output 122 bhp at 6000 rev/min, torque 16.3 kgf.m. (160 lbf.ft) at 4000 rev/min, compression ratio: 9.2:1.
Carburettor: Solex, single.
Clutch: diaphragm, sdp.
Transmission: 4F1R, manual a/s.
Final Drive: rear wheels.
Brakes: disc front, drum rear, servo-assisted.
Steering: worm and roller.
Suspension: coil springs front and rear.
Tyres: 175SR 14.
Dimensions, length: 4620mm (15ft 2.5in); width: 1690mm (5ft 6in); height: 1425mm (4ft 8in); wheelbase: 2636mm (8ft 7in); weight: 1310kg (2889 lb).
Capacities, engine sump: 4.3 litres (7.5 Imp. pints); fuel tank: 70 litres (15.4 Imp. gal); cooling system: 7.1 litres (12.25 Imp. pints).
   Notes: Introduced 1974. Maximum speed 180 km/h (112 mph). Latest version incorporates minor modifications to accommodate increased output from the 2-litre power unit.

BMW (D)

528 i   **2788 cc**

Chassis: unitary construction.
Engine: front-mounted, six-cylinder, in-line, ohc, water-cooled, bore 86mm, stroke 80mm, output 177 bhp at 5800 rev/min, torque 24 kgf.m. (235 lbf.ft.) at 4300 rev/min, compression ratio: 9.0:1.
Carburettor: N.A. (fuel injection).
Clutch: sdp.
Transmission: 4F1R, manual a/s.
Final Drive: rear wheels.
Brakes: disc front and rear, servo-assisted.
Steering: recirculating ball, power-assisted.
Suspension: coil springs front and rear.
Tyres: 195/70HR 14.
Dimensions, length: 4620mm (15ft 2.5in); width: 1690mm (5ft 6in); height: 1425mm (4ft 8in); wheelbase: 2636mm (8ft 7in); weight: 1410 kg (3109 lb).
Capacities, engine sump: 5.8 litres (10.25 Imp. pints); fuel tank: 70 litres (15.4 Imp. gal); cooling system: 12 litres (21 Imp. pints).
   Notes: Top model in the '5-series' range introduced in 1974. Latest 528 (shown) has fuel injection. Also available are the 518 (4-cylinder, 1.7 litre engine), 520 (6-cylinder, 1.9 litre engine) and 525 (6-cylinder, 2.5 litre engine).

BMW (D)

633 Csi   **3210cc**

Chassis: unitary construction.
Engine: front-mounted, six-cylinder, in-line, ohc, water-cooled, bore 89mm, stroke 86mm, output 200 bhp at 5500 rev/min, torque 29 kgf.m. (210 lbf.ft) at 4250 rev/min, compression ratio: 9:1.
Carburettor: Fuel injection.
Clutch: diaphragm, sdp.
Transmission: 4F1R, manual a/s, 3F1R automatic optional.
Final Drive: rear wheels.
Brakes: disc front and rear, servo-assisted.
Steering: ball and nut hydraulic.
Suspension: coil spring front and rear.
Tyres: 195/70VR 14.
Dimensions, length: 4755mm (15ft 7.25in); width: 1725mm (5ft 8in); height: 1365mm (4ft 5.75in); wheelbase: 2626mm (8ft 7in); weight-unladen: 1470 kg (3240 lb).
Capacities, engine sump: 5 litres (8.75 Imp. pints); fuel tank: 70 litres (15.4 Imp. gal); cooling system: 12 litres (21 Imp. pints).
  Notes: Introduced Spring 1976. Specification also includes electronic fuel injection, limited slip differential and transistorized ignition. Also available is the 630 CS with 2986cc engine and Solex carburettor.

BMW (D)

Chassis: unitary construction.
Engine: front-mounted, six-cylinder, in-line, ohc, water-cooled, bore 89mm, stroke 86mm, output 197 bhp at 5500 rev/min, torque 28.3 kgf.m (205 lbf.ft) at 4300 rev/min, compression ratio 9.0:1.
Carburettor: fuel injection.
Clutch: diaphragm, sdp.
Transmission: 4F1R, manual, a/s.
Final Drive: rear wheels.
Brakes: discs front and rear, servo-assisted.
Steering: recirculating ball, power-assisted.
Suspension: coil springs, front and rear.
Tyres: 205/70HR 14.
Dimensions: length: 4877mm (15ft 11.25in); width: 1803mm (5ft 11in); height: 1422mm (4ft 8.25in); wheelbase: 2794mm (9ft 2in); weight: 1600 kg (3528 lb).
Capacities: engine sump: 5.8 litres (10.25 Imp. pints); fuel tank: 85 litres (18.7 Imp. gal); cooling system: 12 litres (21 Imp. pints).

    Notes: Introduced 1977. New luxury '7-series' range which also includes a 728 (6-cylinder, 2.8 litre engine) and 730 (6-cylinder 3.0 litre engine). Technical innovations include seats 'tuned' to the car's springs and shock absorbers, electrically-controlled adjustable rear seats and electronically driven speedometer and rev-counter.

BRISTOL CARS (GB)

603 S   **5900cc**

Chassis: box frame.
Engine: front-mounted, eight-cylinder, V-configuration, ohv, water-cooled, bore 101.6mm, stroke 91mm, compression ratio: 8.4:1.
Carburettor: Carter, single.
Transmission: 3F1R, automatic.
Final Drive: rear wheels.
Brakes: disc front and rear, servo-assisted.
Steering: recirculating ball, power-assisted.
Suspension: independent coil springs front, torsion bars rear.
Tyres: 205VR 15.
Dimensions, length: 4910mm (16ft 1in); width: 1770mm (5ft 9.5in); height: 1440mm (4ft 8.75in); wheelbase: 2900mm (9ft 6in); weight-unladen: 1785 kg (3934 lb).
Capacities, engine sump: 4.8 litres (8.5 Imp. pints); fuel tank: 82 litres (18 Imp. gal); cooling system: 16.5 litres (29 Imp. pints).
  Notes: Introduced October 1976, replacing Bristol 411. Prestige model with aluminium body panels, self-levelling suspension, electronic ignition, 'Speedhold' electronic throttle control, electrically operated front seats, and air-conditioning. Front seat catches release when door is opened. 603E also available powered by 5.2 V-8 engine.

BRISTOL CARS (GB)

412   **6556cc**

Chassis: box frame.
Engine: front-mounted, eight-cylinder, V-configuration, ohv, water-cooled, bore 110mm, stroke 86mm, compression ratio: 8.2:1.
Carburettor: Carter, single.
Transmission: 3F1R, automatic.
Final Drive: rear wheels.
Brakes: disc front and rear, servo-assisted.
Steering: recirculating ball, power-assisted.
Suspension: independent coil spring front, torsion bars rear.
Tyres: 205VR 15.
Dimensions, length: 4940mm (16ft 2.5in); width: 1770mm (5ft 9.5in); height: 1440mm (4ft 8.5in); wheelbase: 2900mm (9ft 6in); weight-unladen 1714 kg (3780 lb).
Capacities, engine sump: 4.8 litres (8.5 Imp. pints); fuel tank: 82 litres (18 Imp. gal); cooling system: 16.5 litres (29 Imp. pints).
   Notes: Introduced January 1976. Two-door convertible saloon. Roof is removable and can be replaced by a canvas roof. Chrysler 6.5 litre engine, self-levelling suspension. 'Speedhold' electronic throttle control.

CHRYSLER (F)

SIMCA 1000 GLS   1118cc

Chassis: unitary construction.
Engine: rear-mounted, four-cylinder, in-line, ohv, water-cooled, bore 74mm, stroke 65mm, output 55 bhp at 6000 rev/min, torque 8.3 kgf.m (59 lbf.ft) at 2600 rev/min, compression ratio: 9.6:1.
Carburettor: Solex, single.
Clutch: sdp.
Transmission: 4F1R, manual a/s.
Final Drive: rear wheels.
Brakes: disc front and rear.
Steering: rack and pinion.
Suspension: independent front with transverse leaf spring.
Tyres: 145 13.
Dimensions, length: 3814mm (12ft 6.25in); width: 1485mm (4ft 10.5in); height: 1365mm (4ft 5.75in); wheelbase: 2220mm (7ft 3.5in); weight-unladen: 802 kg (1768 lb).
Capacities, engine sump: 3 litres (5.3 Imp. pints); fuel tank: 36 litres (8 Imp. gal); cooling system: 6.4 litres (11.3 Imp. pints).
  Notes: The four-door Simca 1000 range features square headlamps and a matt-black front "grille". Also available are the LS with 944cc engine and the SR with 1294cc engine.

CHRYSLER (F)

SIMCA 1100 LX   1118cc

Chassis: unitary construction.
Engine: front-mounted, four-cylinder, in-line, ohv, water-cooled, bore 74mm, stroke 65mm, output 60 bhp at 6000 rev/min, torque 8.6 kgf.m (63 lbf.ft) at 3200 rev/min, compression: 9.6:1.
Carburettor: Solex, single.
Clutch: diaphragm, sdp.
Transmission: 4F1R, manual a/s, optional semi-automatic.
Final Drive: front wheels.
Brakes: disc front, drum rear.
Steering: rack and pinion.
Suspension: independent torsion bars front and rear.
Tyres: 155SR 13.
Dimensions, length: 3931mm (12ft 10.75in); width: 1587mm (5ft 2.5in); height: 1473mm (4ft 10in); wheelbase: 2521mm (8ft. 3¼in.), weight-unladen: 910 kg (2006 lb).
Capacities, engine sump: 3 litres (5.3 Imp. pints); fuel tank: 42 litres (9.25 Imp. gal); cooling system: 5.9 litres (10.5 Imp. pints).
  Notes: The 1100 range which was first introduced in October 1967 comprises the LX (shown), ES LE, GLX and GLS Estate (all with the 1118cc power unit) and the Special (powered by the 1204cc engine).

CHRYSLER (F)

MATRA SIMCA BAGHEERA   1442cc

Chassis: separate frame.
Engine: centrally-mounted, four-cylinder, in-line, ohv, water-cooled, bore 76.7mm, stroke 78mm, output 90 bhp at 5800 rev/min, torque 12.2 kgf.m (88 lbf.ft) at 3200 rev/min, compression ratio: 9.5:1.
Carburettor: Weber, two.
Clutch: sdp.
Transmission: 4F1R, manual, a/s.
Final Drive: rear wheels.
Brakes: disc front and rear, servo-assisted.
Steering: rack and pinion.
Suspension: independent, torsion bars front and rear.
Tyres: 155 13 (front); 185 13 (rear).
Dimensions, length: 4013mm (13ft 2in); width: 1753mm (5ft 8.5in); wheelbase: 2362mm (7ft 9.25in); weight: 1015 kg (2238 lb).
Capacities, engine sump: 3 litres (5.3 Imp. pints); fuel tank: 60 litres (13.2 Imp. gal); cooling system: 10 litres (17.6 Imp. pints).
  Notes: Introduced 1973 (France); and onto the UK market in 1977. Based on the mechanical components of the Simca 1100 and the Chrysler Alpine, this mid-engined, three-seater (abreast), glass-fibre bodied sports model, was developed by Matra with the full co-operation of Chrysler France and is produced at the Matra factory at Romorantin. Top speed for this 1.4 litre engined car is an impressive 113 mph.

CHRYSLER (F)

MATRA SIMCA RANCHO

1442cc

Chassis: unitary construction with separate rear frame.
Engine: front-mounted, four-cylinder, in-line, ohv, water-cooled, bore 76.7mm, stroke 80mm, output 80 bhp at 5600 rev/min, compression ratio 9.5:1.
Carburettor: Weber, single.
Clutch: sdp.
Transmission: 4F1R, manual, a/s.
Final Drive: front wheels.
Brakes: disc front, drum rear, servo-assisted.
Steering: rack and pinion.
Suspension: torsion bars front and rear.
Tyres: 165 14.
Dimension: 4267mm (14ft 0in); width: 1651mm (5ft 5in); height: 1727mm (5ft 8in).
Capacities, engine sump: 3 litres (5.28 Imp. pints); fuel tank: 60 litres (13.20 Imp. gal); cooling system: 6 litres (1.32 Imp. pints).
  Notes: Introduced 1977. Multi-purpose vehicle developed by Matra in conjunction with Chrysler France. Based on the Simca 1100, with the Chrysler Alpine power unit and transmission, this versatile model features a split tailgate, an additional rear seat (rearward facing) and a body comprising normal sheet metal on the front section, and glass fibre reinforced polyester on a metal frame at the rear.

CHRYSLER (F)

2 LITRE **1981cc**

Chassis: unitary construction.
Engine: front-mounted, four-cylinder, in-line, ohc, water-cooled, bore 91.7mm, stroke 75mm, output 110 bhp at 5800 rev/min, torque 16.6 kgf.m (120 lbf.ft) at 3400 rev/min, compression ratio: 9.45:1.
Carburettor: Weber, single.
Clutch: N.A. (auto).
Transmission: 3F1R, automatic.
Final Drive: rear wheels.
Brakes: disc front and rear, servo-assisted.
Steering: rack and pinion.
Suspension: independent coil springs front, coil springs rear.
Tyres: 175 SR 14.
Dimensions, length: 4527mm (14ft 10.25in); width: 1727mm (5ft 8in); height: 1440mm (4ft 8.75in); wheelbase: 2667mm (8ft 9in); weight: 1125 kg (2481 lb).
Capacities, engine sump: 4.5 litres (8 Imp. pints); fuel tank: 64 litres (14.25 Imp. gal); cooling system: 10 litres (17.5 Imp. pints).
   Notes: Introduced 1973 (180: 1970). Designed in Britain and built in Madrid, Spain. Similar to the 180 (1812cc engine) but features the larger engine, automatic transmission as standard and velour covered seats and head restraints.

CHRYSLER (GB)

ALPINE GLS

1442cc

Chassis: unitary construction.
Engine: front-mounted, four-cylinder, in-line, ohv, water-cooled, bore 76.7mm, stroke 78mm, output 85 bhp at 5600 rev/min, torque 12.8 kgf.m (93 lbf.ft) at 3000 rev/min, compression ratio: 9.5:1.
Carburettor: Weber, single.
Clutch: diaphragm, sdp.
Transmission: 4F1R, manual a/s.
Final Drive: front wheels.
Brakes: disc front, drum rear, servo-assisted.
Steering: rack and pinion.
Suspension: independent torsion bars front, independent coil springs rear.
Tyres: 155SR 13.
Dimensions, length: 4245mm (13ft 11in); width: 1680mm (5ft 6in); height: 1400mm (4ft 7in); wheelbase: 2604mm (8ft 6.5in); weight-unladen: 1075 kg (2370 lb).
Capacities, engine sump: 3 litres (5.25 Imp. pints); fuel tank: 60 litres (13 Imp. gal); cooling system: 6.5 litres (11.5 Imp. pints).
  Notes: Introduced 1975. Produced in UK from 1976. Range also includes 1294cc 68 bhp engine. The latest version of the GLS has a number of detail improvements, including a tailgate wash/wipe, additional rear fog light and satin finish instrument surround.

CHRYSLER (GB)

SUNBEAM GL   1598cc

Chassis: unitary construction.
Engine: front-mounted, four-cylinder, in-line, ohc, water-cooled, bore 87.3mm, stroke 66.7mm, output 69 bhp at 4800 rev/min, torque 12.6 kgf.m (91 lbf.ft) at 2900 rev/min, compression ratio: 8.8:1.
Carburettor: Zenith/Stromberg, single.
Clutch: diaphragm, sdp.
Transmission: 4F1R, manual, a/s, 4F1R automatic optional.
Final Drive: rear wheels.
Brakes: disc front, drum rear, servo-assisted.
Steering: rack and pinion.
Suspension: independent coil springs front, coil springs rear.
Tyres: 155-13.
Dimensions, length: 3829mm (12ft 6.75in); width: 1603mm (5ft 3in); height: 1395mm (4ft 7in); wheelbase: 2413mm (7ft 11in); weight: 885 kg (1951 lb).
Capacities, engine sump: 4 litres (7 Imp. pints); fuel tank: 41 litres (9 Imp. gall); cooling system: 7.33 litres (12.9 Imp. pints).
  Notes: Introduced 1977. Three-door, four-seater, hatchback range available with a choice of three engines (930cc, 1300cc, 1598cc) and three levels of trim and equipment (GL shown — and LS and S). The S version is available in the UK only with the 1598cc engine. The all-glass, automatic-lift tailgate gives access to 42.7 cu.ft. of luggage space with rear seats folded.

CHRYSLER (GB)

AVENGER GLS

1589cc

Chassis: unitary construction.
Engine: front-mounted, four-cylinder, in-line, ohv, water-cooled, torque 11.9 kgf.m. (86 lbf.ft) at 4400 rev/min, compression ratio: 8.8:1.
Carburettor: Stromberg, single.
Clutch: diaphragm, sdp.
Transmission: 4F1R, manual a/s, 4F1R automatic optional.
Final Drive: rear wheels.
Brakes: disc front, drum rear, servo-assisted.
Steering: rack and pinion.
Suspension: independent coil spring front, coil spring rear.
Tyres: 155-13.
Dimensions, length: 4267mm (14ft 0in); width: 1613mm (5ft 3.5in); height: 1422mm (4ft 8in); wheelbase: 2489mm (8ft 2in); weight-unladen: 913 kg (2013 lb).
Capacities, engine sump: 4.3 litres (7.5 Imp. pints); fuel tank: 45 litres (10 Imp. gal); cooling system: 7.8 litres (14 Imp. pints).
   Notes: Introduced 1972. Top of the range model. Also available are the Super and Super Estate (1598cc engine) and De Luxe and De Luxe Estate (1295cc engine).
Received modifications to front end and rear light clusters in 1976. Latest version has detail modifications.

CHRYSLER (GB)

HUNTER SUPER   1725cc

Chassis: unitary construction.
Engine: front-mounted, four-cylinder, in-line, ohv, water-cooled, bore 81.5mm, stroke 82.5mm, output 75 bhp at 5100 rev/min, torque 13.1 kgf.m. (95 lbf.ft) at 2500 rev/min, compression ratio: 9.2:1.
Carburettor: Stromberg, single.
Clutch: diaphragm, sdp.
Transmission: 4F1R, manual a/s, 3F1R automatic optional.
Final Drive: rear wheels.
Brakes: disc front, drum rear, servo-assisted.
Steering: recirculating ball.
Suspension: independent coil spring front, leaf spring rear.
Tyres: 155 13.
Dimensions, length: 4343mm (14ft 4in); width: 1613mm (5ft 3.5in); height: 1422mm (4ft 8in); wheelbase: 2501mm (8ft 2in); weight-unladen: 937 kg (2066 lb).
Capacities: engine sump: 4.3 litres (7.5 Imp pints); fuel tank: 45 litres (10 Imp. gal); cooling system: 7.8 litres (14 Imp. pints).
  Notes: Redesignated Chrysler Hunter range comprises Super and De Luxe models. Latest versions feature a distinctive new front grille flanked by four headlamps. The Super (shown) also includes vinyl-covered roof, sports-style road wheels and side repeater flashers.

CHRYSLER (USA)

NEW YORKER BROUGHAM 7210cc

Chassis: unitary construction.
Engine: front-mounted, eight-cylinder, V-configuration, ohv, water-cooled, bore 109.7mm, stroke 95.2mm, output 198 bhp at 3600 rev/min, torque 44.3 kgf.m (320 lbf.ft) at 2000 rev/min, compression ratio 8.2:1.
Carburettor: Carter, single.
Clutch: N.A.
Transmission: 3F1R, automatic.
Final Drive: rear wheels.
Brakes: disc front, drum rear, servo-assisted.
Steering: recirculating ball, power-assisted.
Suspension: independent torsion bars front, leaf springs rear.
Tyres: HR 78 x 15.
Dimensions, length: 5866mm (19ft 4in); width: 2019mm (6ft 7.5in); height: 1384mm (4ft 6.5in); wheelbase: 3150mm (10ft 4in); weight-unladen: 2225 kg (4917 lb).
Capacities, engine sump: 4.7 litres (8.25 Imp. pints); fuel tank: 100 litres (22 Imp. gal); cooling system: 15 litres (26.5 Imp. pints).
  Notes: Flagship of the Chrysler fleet. Four-door hardtop model. Latest version features a new grille and new body side styling features. Two-door hardtop version also available. Newport 2-door and 4-door models are similar.

CITROEN (F)

2 CV6 **602cc**

Chassis: separate frame.
Engine: front-mounted, two-cylinder, horizontally-opposed, ohv, air-cooled, bore 74mm, stroke 70mm, output 33 bhp at 5750 rev/min, torque 4.3 kgf.m (31 lbf.ft) at 4750 rev/min, compression ratio 8.5:1.
Carburettor: Solex, single.
Clutch: sdp.
Transmission: 4F1R, manual, a/s.
Final Drive: front wheels.
Brakes: drum front and rear.
Steering: rack and pinion.
Suspension: independent coil springs front and rear.
Tyres: 125 15.
Dimensions: length: 3800mm (12ft 6.75in); width: 1480in (4ft 10.25in); height: 1585mm (5ft 3in); wheelbase: 2400mm (7ft 10.5in); weight: 559 kg (1232 lb).
Capacities, engine sump: 2.5 litres (4.5 Imp. pints); fuel tank: 20 litres (4.5 Imp. gal).
   Notes: Four-door economy saloon, continued unchanged from previous year. Maximum speed 109 km/h (68 mph).

CITROEN (F)

DYANE 6
602cc

Chassis: separate frame.
Engine: front-mounted, two-cylinder, horizontally opposed, ohv, air-cooled bore 74 mm, stroke 70 mm, output 35 bhp at 5750 rev/min, torque 4.3 kgf.m (31 lbf.ft) at 4750 rev/min, compression ratio 8.5:1.
Carburettor: Solex, single.
Clutch: sdp.
Transmission: 4F1R, manual, a/s.
Final Drive: front wheels.
Brakes: disc front, drum rear.
Steering: rack and pinion.
Suspension: independent, coil springs front and rear.
Tyres: 125 15.
Dimensions, length: 3900mm (12ft 10.75in); width: 1500mm (4ft 11in); height: 1540mm (5ft 1.25in); wheelbase: 2400mm (7ft 10.5in); weight: 595 kg (1312 lb).
Capacities, engine sump: 2.5 litres (4.5 Imp. pints); fuel tank: 25 litres (5.5 Imp. gal).
   Notes: Introduced 1967. Maximum speed 112 km/h (70 mph) approx. Five door hatchback fitted with a sunshine roof. Known in Italy as the Dyanissima. Latest version has front disc brakes and matt black front grille and door handles.

CITROEN (F)

GSX2

1222cc

Chassis: unitary construction.
Engine: front-mounted, four-cylinder, horizontally opposed, ohc, air-cooled, bore 77mm, stroke 65.5mm, output 65 bhp at 5750 rev/min.
Carburettor: Solex single.
Clutch: diaphragm, sdp.
Transmission: 4F1R, manual, a/s.
Final Drive: front wheels.
Brakes: disc front and rear, servo-assisted.
Steering: rack and pinion.
Suspension: independent, hydropneumatic front and rear.
Tyres: Radial ply.
Dimensions, length: 4120mm (13ft 6.25in); width: 1610mm (5ft 3in); height: 1350mm (4ft 5.75in); wheelbase: 2550mm (8ft 4.5in).
Capacities, engine sump: 4.2 litres (7.5 Imp. pints); fuel tank: 43 litres (9.5 Imp. gal).
   Notes: The GS range, which was first introduced in 1970, comprises the GSX2 (shown), G Special (powered by a new 1130cc engine), GS Club, GS Pallas. The latest version of the GSX2 features a number of improvements, including matt black rear spoiler, new wheel trims, fog lamps and interior modifications.

CITROEN (F)

CX GTi

2347cc

Chassis: unitary construction.
Engine: front-mounted, four-cylinder, in-line, ohv, water-cooled, bore 93.5mm, stroke 85.5mm, output 128 bhp at 4800 rev/min, torque 20.1 kgf.m (145.4 lbf.ft) at 3600 rev/min, compression ratio 8.75:1.
Carburettor: N.A. (fuel injection).
Clutch: diaphragm, sdp.
Transmission: 5F1R, manual, a/s.
Final Drive: front wheels.
Brakes: discs front and rear, servo-assisted.
Steering: rack and pinion, power-assisted.
Suspension: hydropneumatic.
Tyres: 185 HR 14.
Dimensions, length: 4670mm (15ft 3.75in); width: 1734mm (5ft 8.25in); height: 1360mm (4ft 5.5in); wheelbase: 2845mm (9ft 4in); weight: unladen 1345 kg (2965 lb).
Capacities, engine sump: 5.8 litres (10.2 Imp. pints); fuel tank: 68 litres (15 Imp. gal).
   Notes: Latest addition to the 'CX' range which was first introduced in and has been added to since 1974 and has production figures in excess of 250,000.
The CX GTi is fitted with Bosch L jetronic fuel injection system and electronic ignition. The CX range now has available three body styles, four engines and five levels of trim. Maximum speed of version shown: 189 kph (118 mph).

COLT (MITSUBISHI) (J)

LANCER 1400   1439cc

Chassis: unitary construction.
Engine: front-mounted, four-cylinder, in-line, ohc, water-cooled, bore 73mm, stroke 86mm, output 68 bhp at 5000 rev/min, torque 10.6 kgf.m (77 lbf.ft) at 3000 rev/min, compression ratio 9.0:1.
Carburettor: Solex, single.
Clutch: diaphragm, sdp.
Transmission: 4F1R, manual a/s; automatic optional on 2-door version.
Final Drive: rear wheels.
Brakes: disc front, drum rear, servo-assisted.
Steering: recirculating ball.
Suspension: independent coil springs front, leaf springs rear.
Tyres: 155 SR x 13.
Dimensions, length: 3995mm (13ft 1.5in); width: 1535mm (5ft 5in); height: 1360mm (4ft 5.5in); wheelbase: 2340mm (7ft 8.25in).
Capacities, engine sump: 4.5 litres (8 Imp. pints); fuel tank: 50 litres (11 Imp. gal); cooling system: 6 litres (10.5 Imp. pints).
   Notes: Introduced 1973 (Japan). Latest range, available as 1200, 1400 saloon (2- and 4-door) and estate, and 1600 Sport GSR, features new front grille, modified rear end and improved interior. The 1600 Sport (East African Safari winner) is fitted with the "Saturn 80" engine as used in the Celeste and Sigma models.

COLT (MITSUBISHI) (J)

CELESTE 1600 GS   1597cc

Chassis: unitary construction.
Engine: front-mounted, four-cylinder, in-line, ohc, water-cooled, bore 76.9mm, stroke 90mm, output 94 bhp at 6200 rev/min, torque 12.8 kgf.m (92.5 lbf.ft) at 4200 rev/min, compression ratio: 9.5:1.
Carburettor: Solex, twin.
Clutch: diaphragm, sdp.
Transmission: 5F1R, manual, a/s.
Final Drive: rear wheels.
Brakes: disc front, drum rear, servo-assisted.
Steering: recirculating ball.
Suspension: independent coil springs front, leaf springs rear.
Tyres: 175 + 70 HR x 13.
Dimensions, length: 4115mm (13ft 6in); width: 1610mm (5ft 3.5in); height: 1330mm (4ft 4.5in); wheelbase: 2340mm (7ft 8.25in); weight-unladen: 930 kg (2050 lb).
Capacities, engine sump: 4.5 litres (8 Imp. pints); fuel tank: 45 litres (10 Imp. gal); cooling system: 6 litres (10.5 Imp. pints).
  Notes: Latest edition to the Celeste range which also includes the 1600 ST (less powerful 1597cc engine) and 2000 GT (1995cc engine). Three-door hatchback design. Maximum speed 163 km/h (102 mph).

COLT (MITSUBISHI) (J)

SIGMA 2000   1995cc

Chassis: unitary construction.
Engine: front-mounted, four-cylinder, in-line, ohc, water-cooled, bore 84mm, stroke 90mm, output 98 bhp at 6000 rev/min, torque 16.7 kgf.m at 4000 rev/min, compression ratio: 9.0:1.
Carburettor: Solex, single.
Clutch: diaphragm, sdp.
Transmission: 5F1R, manual, a/s; automatic optional.
Final Drive: rear wheels.
Brakes: disc front, drum rear.
Steering: recirculating ball.
Suspension: independent coil springs front, coil springs rear.
Tyres: 165 SR 13.
Dimensions, length: 4330mm (14ft 2in); width: 1655mm (5ft 5.25in); height: 1360mm (4ft 5.5in); wheelbase: 2515mm (8ft 3in); weight-unladen: 952 kg (2100 lb).
Capacities, engine sump: 4.5 litres (8 Imp. pints); fuel tank: 60 litres (13.25 Imp. gal); cooling system: 6 litres (10.5 Imp. pints).
   Notes: Introduced 1976 (GB). Most recent Colt model, also available as 1600 (1597cc, 85 bhp engine). Features front spoiler, twin headlamps, tinted glass and, on the 2000, reclining front and rear seats.

DATSUN (J)

CHERRY 100A F11   988cc

Chassis: unitary construction.
Engine: front-mounted, four-cylinder, in-line, ohv, water-cooled,
bore 73mm, stroke 59mm, output 45 bhp at 5600 rev/min,
torque 7.7 kgf.m (55.7 lbf.ft) at 4000 rev/min, compression
ratio: 9.0:1.
Carburettor: Hitachi, single.
Clutch: diaphragm, sdp.
Transmission: 4F1R, manual, a/s.
Final Drive: front wheels.
Brakes: disc front, drum rear, servo-assisted.
Steering: rack and pinion.
Suspension: independent coil springs, front and rear.
Tyres: 6.00S 12.
Dimensions, length: 3810mm (12ft 6.5in); width: 1499mm (4ft
11in); height: 1295mm (4ft 3in); wheelbase: 2388mm (7ft 10.25in);
weight: 715 kg (1575 lb).
Capacities, engine sump: 3.3 litres (5.8 Imp. pints); fuel tank:
40 litres (8.8 Imp. gal); cooling system: 5.5 litres (9.8 Imp. pints).
   Notes: Introduced 1971. Latest F11 range, comprising seven
models (three 2-door saloons, a 4-door saloon, two 3-door estates
and a 120A 3-door coupé), features restyled bodywork and various
mechanical and interior modifications.

DATSUN (J)

SUNNY 120Y Coupé   **1171cc**

Chassis: unitary construction.
Engine: front-mounted, four-cylinder, in-line, ohv, water-cooled, bore 73mm, stroke 70mm, output 65 bhp at 6000 rev/min, torque 9.4 kgf.m (68 lbf.ft) at 3600 rev/min, compression ratio: 9.0:1.
Carburettor: Hitachi, single.
Clutch: diaphragm, sdp.
Transmission: 4F1R, manual, a/s.
Final Drive: rear wheels.
Brakes: disc front, drum rear, servo-assisted.
Steering: recirculating ball.
Suspension: independent coil springs front, leaf springs rear.
Tyres: 155 SR 13.
Dimensions, length: 3950mm (12ft 11.5in); width: 1549mm (5ft 1in); height: 1372mm (4ft 6in); wheelbase: 2337mm (7ft 8in); weight: 808kg (1782 lb).
Capacities, engine sump: 3.3 litres (5.8 Imp. pints); fuel tank: 43 litres (9.5 Imp. gal); cooling system: 4.8 litres (8.5 Imp. pints).
   Notes: Available as Coupé (shown), GLS 2- and 4-door Saloons and Estate. Standard specification includes tinted glass all-round, reclining front cloth seats, head restraints, radio and clock.

DATSUN (J)

BLUEBIRD 180B SSS Coupé   1770cc

Chassis: unitary construction.
Engine: front-mounted, four-cylinder, in-line, ohc, water-cooled, bore 85mm, stroke 78mm, output 90 bhp at 5800 rev/min, torque 13.9 kgf.m (100.5 lbf.ft) at 3800 rev/min, compression ratio: 8.5:1.
Carburettor: SU, two.
Clutch: diaphragm, sdp.
Transmission: 5F1R, manual, a/s.
Final Drive: rear wheels.
Brakes: disc front, drum rear, servo-assisted.
Steering: recirculating ball.
Suspension: independent coil springs front and rear.
Tyres: 185/70 HR 14.
Dimensions, length: 4267mm (13ft 11.75in); width: 1626mm (5ft 4.25in); height: 1372mm (4ft 6.25in); wheelbase: 2489mm (8ft 2.5in); weight: 1065 kg (2348 lb).
Capacities, engine sump: 4.3 litres (7.5 Imp. pints); fuel tank: 56 litres (12.3 Imp. gal); cooling system: 6.5 litres (11.3 Imp. pints).
  Notes: Introduced 1972. Latest Mark II version which features restyled bodywork and interior, is available as 4-door Saloon, 5-door Estate and SSS 2-door Sports Coupé (shown).

DATSUN (J)

LAUREL SIX

1998cc

Chassis: unitary construction.
Engine: front-mounted, six-cylinder, in-line, ohc, water-cooled, bore 78mm, stroke 69.7mm, output 100 bhp at 5600 rev/min, torque 14.5 kgf.m (105 lbf.ft) at 3600 rev/min, compression ratio: 8.6:1.
Carburettor: Hitachi, single.
Clutch: diaphragm, sdp.
Transmission: 4F1R, manual, a/s; 3F1R automatic optional.
Final Drive: rear wheels.
Brakes: disc front, drum rear, servo-assisted.
Steering: recirculating ball.
Suspension: independent coil springs front, coil springs rear.
Tyres: 185/70 HR 14.
Dimensions, length: 4510mm (14ft 10in); width: 1683mm (5ft 6.25in); height: 1410mm (4ft 7.5in); wheelbase: 2670mm (8ft 9in); weight: 1180 kg (2601 lb).
Capacities, engine sump: 5.7 litres (10 Imp. pints); fuel tank: 60 litres (13.25 Imp. gal); cooling system: 9.1 litres (14.75 Imp. pints).

Notes: Introduced 1974. Latest version of this 4-door Saloon has a restyled body, with lower waistline, larger windows and increased space for passengers and luggage. Other modifications include new rear suspension and improved interior and instrumentation. Maximum speed 103 mph.

DATSUN (J)

260Z   **2565cc**

Chassis: unitary construction.
Engine: front-mounted, six-cylinder, in-line, ohc, water-cooled, bore 83 mm, stroke 79 mm, output 150 bhp at 5400 rev/min, torque 21.9 kgf.m (158 lbf.ft) at 4400 rev/min, compression ratio 8.3:1.
Carburettor: Hitachi, twin.
Clutch: diaphragm, sdp.
Transmission: 5F1R, manual, a/s.
Final Drive: rear wheels.
Brakes: disc front, drum rear, servo-assisted.
Steering: rack and pinion.
Suspension: independent coil springs front and rear.
Tyres: 195/70VR 14.
Dimensions, length: 4115mm (13ft 6in); width: 1632mm (5ft 4.25in); height: 1282mm (4ft 2.5in); wheelbase: 2305mm (7ft 6.75in); weight: 1130 kg (2491 lb).
Capacities, engine sump: 4 litres (7 Imp. pints); fuel tank: 65 litres (14.25 Imp. gal); cooling system: 9.5 litres (16.75 Imp. pints).
   Notes: Introduced 1973. Top selling sports car, reintroduced in the U.K. after a three year absence. Two-seater with top speed of around 203 km/h (127 mph). 260Z 2 + 2 version also available.

FERRARI (I)

308 GTB   **2926cc**

Chassis: separate frame.
Engine: centre-mounted, eight-cylinder, V-configuration, ohc, water-cooled, bore 81mm, stroke 71mm, output 255 bhp at 7700 rev/min, torque 29 kgf.m (209 lb.ft) at 5000 rev/min, compression ratio: 8.8:1.
Carburettor: Weber, four.
Clutch: diaphragm, sdp.
Transmission: 5F1R, manual, a/s.
Final Drive: rear wheels.
Brakes: disc front and rear, servo-assisted.
Steering: rack and pinion.
Suspension: independent coil spring front and rear.
Tyres: 205/70VR 14.
Dimensions, length: 4230mm (13ft 10.5in); width: 1720mm (5ft 7.75in); height: 1200mm (3ft 8in); wheelbase: 2340mm (7ft 8in); weight-unladen 1090 kg (2403 lb).
Capacities, engine sump: 9 litres (16 Imp. pints); fuel tank: 80 litres (17.5 Imp. gal); cooling system: 18 litres (31.5 Imp. pints).
Notes: Maximum speed 250 km/h (155 mph). Mechanically similar to Dino 308 but with body designed by Pininfarina. Limited slip differential incorporated in the gearbox. Specification includes pop-up headlamps.

DINO 308 GT4 2 + 2   2926cc

Chassis: separate frame.
Engine: centre-mounted, eight-cylinder, V-configuration, ohc, water-cooled, bore 81mm, stroke 71mm, output 255 bhp at 7700 rev/min, torque 29 kgf.m (209 lbf.ft) at 5000 rev/min, compression ratio: 8.8:1.
Carburettor: Weber, four.
Clutch: diaphragm, sdp.
Transmission: 5F1R, manual, a/s.
Final Drive: rear wheels.
Brakes: disc front and rear, servo-assisted.
Steering: rack and pinion.
Suspension: independent coil spring front and rear.
Tyres: 205/70VR 14.
Dimensions, length: 4300mm (14ft 1.25in); width: 1800mm (5ft 11in); height: 1180mm (3ft 10.5in); wheelbase: 2550mm (8ft 4.5in); weight-unladen: 1150 kg (2526 lb).
Capacities, engine sump: 9 litres (16 Imp. pints); fuel tank: 80 litres (17.5 Imp. gal); cooling system: 18 litres (31.5 Imp. pints).
   Notes: Two-door 2 + 2 with a top speed of 250 km/h (155 mph). Designed by Bertone. Limited slip differential incorporated in the gearbox. Air-conditioning is optionally available.

FERRARI (I)

400 GT Automatic
4823cc

Chassis: separate frame.
Engine: front-mounted, twelve-cylinder, V-configuration, ohc, water-cooled, bore 81mm, stroke 78mm, rev/min, torque 48 kgf.m. (347lbf.ft) at 3600 rev/min, compression ratio: 8.8:1.
Carburettor: Weber, six.
Clutch: sdp.
Transmission: 3F1R, automatic; 5F1R manual optional.
Final Drive: rear wheels.
Brakes: disc front and rear, servo-assisted.
Steering: rack and pinion, power-assisted.
Suspension: independent coil springs front and rear.
Tyres: 215/70 VR 15.
Dimensions, length: 4810mm (15ft 9.5in); width: 1798mm (5ft 11in); height: 1314mm (4ft 3.5in); wheelbase: 2692mm (8ft 10.25in); weight: 1900 kg (4180 lb).
Capacities, engine sump: 18.5 litres (32.5 Imp. pints); fuel tank: 120 litres (26.5 Imp. gal); cooling system: 15 litres (26.5 Imp. pints).
   Notes: Maximum speed 149 mph. Features a limited slip differential. Air conditioning, electric windows and radio fitted as standard. Manual version also available.

FERRARI (I)

512 BB   **4942cc**

Chassis: separate frame.
Engine: centre-mounted, twelve-cylinder, horizontally-opposed, ohc, water-cooled, bore 82mm, stroke 78mm, output 360 bhp at 6800 rev/min, torque 46 kgf.m (332 lbf.ft) at 4600 rev/min, compression ratio: 9.2:1.
Carburettor: Weber, four.
Clutch: ddp.
Transmission: 5F1R, manual, a/s.
Final Drive: rear wheels.
Brakes: disc front and rear, servo-assisted.
Steering: rack and pinion.
Suspension: independent coil springs front and rear.
Tyres: 215/70 VR 15 front; 225/70 VR 15 (rear).
Dimensions, length: 4394mm (14ft 5.25in); width: 1829mm (6ft 0in); height: 1118mm (3ft 8in); wheelbase: 2489mm (8ft 2.5in); weight: 1399kg (3084 lb).
Capacities, engine sump: 13 litres (22.8 Imp pints); fuel tank: 120 litres (26.4 Imp. gal); cooling system: 22 litres (38.5 Imp. pints).
  Notes: Maximum speed 304 km/h (188 mph). Features flat-12 engine, rear mounted gearbox and a limited-slip differential incorporated in the final drive unit. Air conditioning and electric windows fitted as standard.

FIAT (I)

126 DeVille   **549cc**

Chassis: unitary construction.
Engine: rear-mounted, two-cylinder, in-line, ohv, air-cooled, bore 73.5mm, stroke 70mm, output 23 bhp at 4800 rev/min, torque 4 kgf.m (29 lbf.ft) at 3400 rev/min, compression ratio: 7.5:1.
Carburettor: Weber, single.
Clutch: diaphragm, sdp.
Transmission: 4F1R, manual a/s.
Final Drive: rear wheels.
Brakes: drum front and rear.
Steering: worm and sector.
Suspension: independent leaf spring front, independent coil spring rear.
Tyres: 135 SR 12.
Dimensions, length: 3124mm (10ft 3.25in); width: 1385mm (4ft 6.5in); height: 1330mm (4ft 4.25in); wheelbase: 1840mm (6ft 0.75in); weight-unladen: 580 kg (1278 lb).
Capacities, engine sump: 2.5 litres (4.5 Imp. pints); fuel tank: 21 litres (4.5 Imp. gal).
  Notes: Introduced 1972. (De Ville 1977). Available as Saloon and De Ville (shown). The De Ville standard equipment specification includes sun-roof, reclining front seats, moulded resin bumpers, and rubber side strips. Maximum speed 104 km/h (65 mph).

61

Chassis: unitary construction.
Engine: front-mounted, four-cylinder, in-line, ohc, water-cooled, bore 76mm, stroke 57.8mm, output 50 bhp at 5600 rev/min, torque 7.9 kgf.m (57.1 lbf.ft) at 3000 rev/min, compression ratio: 9.3:1.
Carburettor: Weber or Solex, single.
Clutch: diaphragm, sdp.
Transmission: 4F1R, manual, a/s.
Final Drive: rear wheels.
Brakes: disc front, drum rear.
Steering: rack and pinion.
Suspension: independent coil springs front, leaf springs rear.
Tyres: 135 SR x 13.
Dimensions, length: 3595mm (11ft 9.3in); width: 1527mm (5ft 0in); height: 1370mm (4ft 6in); wheelbase: 2225mm (7ft 3.8in); weight: 708 kg (1561 lb).
Capacities, engine sump: 2.8 litres (4.75 Imp. pints); fuel tank: 30 litres (6.5 Imp. gal); cooling system: 5.5 litres (9.5 Imp. pints).
  Notes: Introduced 1971 (new version 1977). Latest restyled model features rectangular headlamps in a new radiator grille, larger windows, moulded resin front bumper and rubber side trims. The new 1050cc engine, which is produced in Brazil, is optional to the proven 903cc unit. The range to be marketed in the U.K. comprises four models: 900L, C and CL and 1050CL.

FIAT (I)

Chassis: unitary construction.
Engine: front-mounted, four-cylinder, in-line, ohc, water-cooled, bore 86mm, stroke 55.5mm, output 60 bhp at 6000 rev/min, compression ratio: 9.2:1.
Carburettor: Weber, single.
Clutch: diaphragm, sdp.
Transmission: 4F1R, manual a/s.
Final Drive: front wheels.
Brakes: disc front, drum rear, servo-assisted.
Steering: rack and pinion.
Suspension: independent coil spring front, leaf spring rear.
Tyres: 145SR 13.
Dimensions, length: 3657mm (12ft 0in); width: 1587mm (5ft 2.5in); height: 1422mm (4ft 8in); wheelbase: 2451mm (8ft 0.5in); weight-unladen: 815 kg (1818 lb).
Capacities, engine sump: 4.25 litres (7.5 Imp. pints); fuel tank: 38 litres (8.5 Imp. gal); cooling system: 6.5 litres (11.5 Imp. pints).
   Notes: First introduced in the UK in 1970. Latest 128 range comprises four models (saloons and estates — C and CL versions). The Fiat Berlinetta 3-door coupé is fitted with a more powerful version of the 1290cc engine (73 bhp).

FIAT (I)

X1/9   **1290cc**

Chassis: unitary construction.
Engine: rear-mounted, four-cylinder, in-line, ohc, water-cooled, bore 86mm, stroke 55.5mm, output 73 bhp at 6600 rev/min, torque 9.9 kgf.m (71.6 lbf.ft) at 3400 rev/min, compression ratio: 9.2:1.
Carburettor: Weber, single.
Clutch: diaphragm, sdp.
Transmission: 4F1R, manual a/s.
Final Drive: rear wheels.
Brakes: discs front and rear.
Steering: rack and pinion.
Suspension: independent coil springs, front and rear.
Tyres: 145HR 13.
Dimensions: length: 3830mm (12ft 7in); width: 1575mm (5ft 2in); height: 1170mm (3ft 10in); wheelbase: 2200mm (7ft 2.5in); weight-unladen: 880 kg (1940 lb).
Capacities, engine sump: 4.25 litres (7.5 Imp. pints); fuel tank: 48 litres (10.5 Imp. gal); cooling system: 10.5 litres (18.5 Imp. pints).
   Notes: Introduced 1972. Maximum speed 169 km/h (105 mph) approximately. Bertone styled body, two-seater sports car with removable roof, concealed headlamps and front air spoiler.

FIAT (I)

MIRAFIORI 1600 Special Estate   1585cc

Chassis: unitary construction.
Engine: front-mounted, four-cylinder, in-line, ohv, water-cooled, bore 84mm, stroke 71.5mm, output 75 bhp at 5400 rev/min, torque 12.6 kgf.m (91 lbf.ft) at 3000 rev/min, compression ratio: 9.2:1.
Carburettor: Weber, single.
Clutch: diaphragm, sdp.
Transmission: 4F1R, manual a/s, 5F1R or automatic optional.
Final Drive: rear wheels.
Brakes: disc front, drum rear, servo-assisted.
Steering: rack and pinion.
Suspension: independent coil springs front, coil spring rear.
Tyres: 155SR13.
Dimensions, length: 4264mm (14ft 0in); width: 1642mm (5ft 5in); height: 1400mm (4ft 7in); wheelbase: 2490mm (8ft 2in); weight-unladen: 995 kg (2194 lb).
Capacities, engine sump: 3.7 litres (6.5 Imp. pints); fuel tank: 50 litres (11 Imp. gal); cooling system: 7.4 litres (13 Imp. pints).
   Notes: Introduced 1974. Current range comprises the 1600 Special Saloon and Estate (shown). 1300 2-door and 4-door Saloons also available (powered by a 1297cc, 65 bhp engine).

132 "2000"   **1995cc**

Chassis: unitary construction.
Engine: front-mounted, four-cylinder, in-line, ohc, water-cooled, bore 84mm, stroke 90mm, output 112 bhp at 5600 rev/min, torque 16.1 kgf.m (116 lbf.ft) at 3000 rev/min, compression ratio: 8.9:1.
Carburettor: Weber, single.
Clutch: diaphragm, sdp.
Transmission: 5F1R, manual, a/s.
Final Drive: rear wheels.
Brakes: disc front, drum rear, servo-assisted.
Steering: recirculating ball, power assisted.
Suspension: independent coil springs front, coil springs rear.
Tyres: 175/70 SR 14.
Dimensions, length: 4405mm (14ft 5in); width: 1640mm (5ft 4.5in); height: 1425mm (4ft 8in); wheelbase: 2557mm (8ft 4.25in); weight: 1100 kg (2425 lb).
Capacities, engine sump: 3.3 litres (5.8 Imp. pints); fuel tank: 55.9 litres (12.3 Imp. gal); cooling system: 8 litres (14.1 Imp. pints).
  Notes: Introduced in 1977 to replace the 132 1800 ES and 1600 GLS models, this flagship of the FIAT range is distinguishable by moulded rubber side strips, new radiator grille with twin headlamps, flexible resin bumpers and special wheel trims.
Also featured are a new 2.0 litre power unit and completely restyled interior.

FORD (GB/D)

ESCORT 1300 GL   1297cc

Chassis: unitary construction.
Engine: front-mounted, four-cylinder, in-line, ohv, water-cooled, bore 80.98mm, stroke 62.99 mm, output 57 bhp at 5500 rev/min, torque 68 lbf.ft (9.3 kgf.m) at 3000 rev/min, compression ratio 9.2:1.
Carburettor: Ford, single.
Clutch: diaphragm, sdp.
Transmission: 4F1R manual a/s, optional 3F1R automatic.
Final Drive: rear wheels.
Brakes: disc front, drum rear, servo-assisted.
Steering: rack and pinion.
Suspension: independent coil springs front, leaf springs rear.
Tyres: 155SR 13.
Dimensions, length: 3975mm (13ft 0.5 in); width: 1593mm (5ft 2.75in); height: 1408mm (4ft 6.5in); wheelbase: 2400mm (7ft 10.5in); weight-unladen: 881 kg (1940 lb).
Capacities, engine sump: 3.25 litres (5.7 Imp. pints); fuel tank: 41 litres (9 Imp. gal); cooling system: 5 litres (8.8 Imp. pints).
  Notes: Re-styled Escort announced in January 1975. Available engines also include 1097cc, 1598cc, 1843cc and 1993cc. The 'Popular' and 'Popular Plus' models are available in the U.K. only.

FORD (GB/D)

CAPRI GHIA

2994cc

Chassis: unitary construction.
Engine: front-mounted, six-cylinder, V-configuration, ohv, water-cooled, bore 93.67mm, stroke 72.4mm, output 138 bhp at 5000 rev/min, torque 24 kgf.m (174 lbf.ft) at 3000 rev/min, compression ratio 9.0:1.
Carburettor: Ford, single.
Clutch: diaphragm, sdp.
Transmission: 3F1R, automatic.
Final Drive: rear wheels.
Brakes: disc front, drum rear, servo-assisted.
Steering: rack and pinion, power-assisted.
Suspension: independent coil springs front, leaf springs rear.
Tyres: 185 HR/70 x 13.
Dimensions, length: 4318mm (14ft 2in); width: 1698mm (5ft 7in); height: 1353mm (4ft 5.25in); wheelbase: 2565mm (8ft 5in); weight-unladen: 1168 kg (2574 lb).
Capacities, engine sump: 5 litres (8.75 Imp. pints); fuel tank: 58 litres (12.75 Imp. gal); cooling system: 9.3 litres (16.5 Imp. pints).
  Notes: Introduced 1974 (Capri Mk 1 range 1969). Top model in the range featuring vinyl roof, light alloy road wheels, sunshine roof with tilting device, tinted glass and special interior trim. Also available are Capri 1300, L, GL, S and a 2-litre engined Ghia.

FORD (GB/D)

CORTINA 'S'

2294cc

Chassis: unitary construction.
Engine: front-mounted, six-cylinder, V-configuration, ohv, water-cooled, bore 90mm, stroke 60.1mm, output 108 bhp at 5000 rev/min, compression ratio 8.75:1.
Carburettor: Ford, single.
Clutch: diaphragm, sdp.
Transmission: 4F1R, manual, a/s.
Final Drive: rear wheels.
Brakes: disc front, drum rear, servo-assisted.
Steering: rack and pinion, power assisted.
Suspension: independent coil springs front, coil springs rear.
Tyres: 165 SR13.
Dimensions, length: 4348mm (14ft 2.5in); width: 1702mm (5ft 7in); height: 1358mm (4ft 5.5in); wheelbase: 2578mm (9ft 5.5in); weight: 1130 kg (2492 lb).
Capacities, engine sump: 4.5 litres (7.9 Imp. pints); fuel tank: 54 litres (12 Imp. gal); cooling system: 6.9 litres (12.1 Imp. pints).
   Notes: Restyled range, which replaced the Mk. III in 1976, is continued with a number of detail changes. Choice ranges from the 1300 two-door version to the luxurious Ghia. The 'S' model shown is powered by a new 6-cylinder, lightweight engine previously available on the German sister Taunus models.

FORD (GB/D)

GRANADA GHIA

2792cc

Chassis: unitary construction.
Engine: front-mounted, six-cylinder, v-configuration, ohv, water-cooled, bore 93mm, stroke 68.5mm, output 135 bhp at 5200 rev/min, torque 00 kgf.m (159 lbf.ft) at 3000 rev/min, compression ratio 9.2:1.
Carburettor: Solex, single (fuel inj. opt.).
Clutch: diaphragm, sdp.
Transmission: 3F1R, automatic; 4F1R manual optional.
Final drive: rear wheels.
Brakes: disc front, drum rear, servo-assisted.
Steering: rack and pinion, power-assisted.
Suspension: independent coil springs front and rear.
Tyres: 185 SR14.
Dimensions: length 4736mm (15ft 7in); width: 1791mm (5ft 10.5in); height: 1378mm (4ft 6.25in); wheelbase: 2769mm (9ft 1in); weight: 1370 kg (3009 lb).
Capacities, engine sump: 4.3 litres (7.5 Imp. pints); fuel tank: 65 litres (14.3 Imp. gal); cooling system: 10.2 litres (18 Imp. pints).
   Notes: Latest revisions to the Granada range — first introduced in 1972 — include modified body styling, new range of V-6 engines (including 2.1 litre diesel), improved suspension and numerous other modifications/refinements. The top-of-the-range Ghia (shown) has alloy wheels, sunroof, electrically-operating front windows, and radio/stereo cassette player as standard.

FORD (GB/D/E)

FIESTA

1298cc

Chassis: unitary construction.
Engine: front-mounted, four-cylinder, in-line, ohv, water-cooled, bore 81mm, stroke 63mm, output 66 bhp at 5600 rev/min, torque 9.4 kgf.m (68 lbf.ft) at 3250 rev/min, compression ratio 9.2:1.
Carburettor: Weber, single.
Clutch: diaphragm sdp.
Transmission: 4F1R, manual, a/s.
Final Drive: front wheels.
Brakes: disc front, drum rear, servo assistance optional.
Steering: rack and pinion.
Suspension: independent coil springs front, coil springs rear.
Tyres: 155 SR12.
Dimensions: length: 3565mm (11ft 8.4in); width: 1567mm (5ft 1.7in); height: 1314mm (4ft 3.7in); wheelbase: 2286mm (7ft 6in); weight: 730 kg (1606 lb).
Capacities, engine sump: 3.25 litres (5.7 Imp pints); fuel tank: 34 litres (7.5 Imp. gal); cooling system: 6.2 litres (10.9 Imp. pints).
   Notes: Introduced 1976 (1977 in UK). Built at Dagenham, UK, Saarlouis, Germany and Valencia, Spain, this front-wheel drive mini-car range has been extended by the recent introduction of 1300, hatchback, 'S' and Ghia models, which are powered by a modified version of the engine fitted to the Escort Sport and Ghia models. The increased performance has necessitated modifications to suspension, brakes and final drive. Rear wing numerals ('S' version) and tailgate badge (Ghia version) identify these larger-engined versions.

FORD (USA)

MERCURY MONARCH GHIA

4950cc

Engine: front-mounted, eight-cylinder, V-configuration, ohv, water-cooled, bore 101.6mm, stroke 76.2mm, output 139 bhp at 3600 rev/min, torque 34.57 kgf.m (250 lbf.ft) at 1600 rev/min, compression ratio: 8.4:1.
Carburettor: FORD 2150A Downdraft (Except California).
Clutch: sdp.
Transmission: 4F1R, + overdrive a/s, 3-speed Automatic optional.
Final Drive: rear wheels.
Brakes: disc front, drum rear.
Steering: recirculating ball and nut.
Suspension: independent coil springs front, semi-elliptical leaf springs rear.
Tyres: Radial ply.
Dimensions, length: 5022mm (16ft 5.75in); width: 1880mm (6ft 1.75in); height: 1351mm (4ft 5.75in); wheelbase: 2791mm (9ft 2in); weight: 1482 kg (3268 lb).
Capacities, engine sump: 5.7 litres (10 Imp. pints); fuel tank: 68 litres (15 Imp. gal); cooling system: 16 litres (28 Imp. pints).
Notes: Available in right-hand drive form as 2-door Coupe and 4-door Saloon, both with Ghia and ESS options. Automatic speed control, power seats, central locking system and "moon roof" are other available options. 6-cylinder in-line engine also available.

FORD MOTORS (USA)

FAIRMONT 4950cc

Engine: front-mounted, eight-cylinder, V-configuration, ohv, water-cooled, bore 101.6mm, stroke 76.2mm, output 139 bhp at 3600 rev/min, torque 34.57 kgf.m (250 lbf.ft) at 1600 rev/min, compression ratio: 8.4:1.
Carburettor: Ford Downdraft.
Clutch: sdp.
Transmission: 4F1R, manual a/s.
Final Drive: rear wheels.
Brakes: disc front, drum rear.
Steering: rack and pinion.
Suspension: independent front; four bar link; coils, rear.
Tyres: Radial Ply.
Dimensions: length: 4923mm (16ft 1.75in); width: 1803mm (5ft 11in); height: 1392mm (4ft 6.75in); wheelbase: 2680mm (8ft 9.5in); weight: 1306 kg (2879 lb).
Capacities, engine sump: 5.7 litres (10 Imp. pints); fuel tank: 60 litres (13.25 Imp. gal); cooling system: 16 litres (28 Imp. pints).
   Notes: This 4-door Station Wagon, available in right-hand drive form provides 79.5 cubic feet of cargo space. Figures quoted are for the 302 CID engine. 140 CID and 200 CID power units are available as options.

FORD (MOTORS (USA)

MUSTANG II GHIA

4950cc

Engine: front-mounted, eight-cylinder, V-configuration, ohv, water-cooled, bore 101.6mm, stroke 76.2mm, output 139 bhp at 3600 rev/min, torque 34.57 kgf.m (250 lbf.ft) at 1600 rev/min, compression ratio: 8.4:1.

Carburettor: Downdraft.

Clutch: sdp.

Transmission: 4F1R, manual a/s, Ford C4 Automatic optional.

Final Drive: rear wheels.

Brakes: disc front, drum rear.

Steering: rack and pinion.

Suspension: independent front, Semi-elliptical leaf spring, rear.

Tyres: Steel Belted Radial.

Dimensions, length: 4445mm (14ft 7in); width: 1784mm (5ft 10.25in); height: 1276mm (4ft 2.5in); wheelbase: 2438mm (8ft 0in); weight: 1210 kg (2736 lb).

Capacities, engine sump: 5.7 litres (10 Imp. pints); fuel tank: 62.5 litres (13.75 Imp. gal); cooling system: 16 litres (28 Imp. pints).

Notes: This is one of Britains favourite "transatlantic" cars. The 1978 version in right hand drive Ghia form has a vinyl half roof and is powered by the 5-litre V8 engine coupled to the Ford C4 Automatic Transmission.

GENERAL MOTORS (USA)

CHEVROLET CAPRICE CLASSIC **4096cc**

Chassis: separate frame.
Engine: front-mounted, six-cylinder, in-line, ohv, water-cooled, bore 98.4mm, stroke 89.7mm, output 82 bhp at 3800 rev/min, torque 19.5 kgf.m (264 lbf.ft) at 1600 rev/min, compression ratio: 8.1:1.
Carburettor: Rochester, single.
Clutch: N.A.
Transmission: 3F1R, automatic.
Final Drive: rear wheels.
Brakes: drums front and rear, servo-assisted.
Steering: recirculating ball, power assisted.
Suspension: independent coil springs front, coil springs rear.
Tyres: FR78 x 15.
Dimensions, length: 5385mm (17ft 8in); width: 1930mm (6ft 4in); height: 1422mm (4ft 8in); wheelbase: 2945mm (9ft 8in); weight-unladen: 1672 kg (3695 lb).
Capacities, engine sump: 3.8 litres (7 Imp. pints); fuel tank: 79.5 litres (17.5 Imp. gal); cooling system: 13.4 litres 7.5 Imp. pints).
   Notes: Redesigned in 1976, this model is continued with front and rear end modifications. Available as four-door Sedan (shown), two-door Coupé and four-door Station Wagon. Alternative engines available: 5 litre V-8 and 5.7 litre V-8.

GENERAL MOTORS (USA)

CHEVROLET CORVETTE   5735cc

Chassis: separate frame.
Engine: front-mounted, eight-cylinder, V-configuration, ohv,
water-cooled, bore 101.6mm, stroke 88.4mm, output 185 bhp
at 4000 rev/min, torque 38.7 kgf.m (280 lbf.ft) at 2400 rev/
min, compression ratio: 8.2:1.
Carburettor: Rochester, single.
Clutch: N.A.
Transmission: 4F1R, manual, a/s; 3F1R automatic optional.
Final Drive: rear wheels.
Brakes: disc front and rear, servo-assisted.
Steering: recirculating ball, power-assisted.
Suspension: independent coil springs front, independent
transverse leaf spring rear.
Tyres: P 225/70R15.
Dimensions, length: 4705mm (15ft 5.25in); width: 1750mm
(5ft 9in); height: 1220mm (4ft 0in); wheelbase: 2490mm
(8ft 2in); weight-unladen: 1621 kg (3572 lb).
Capacities, engine sump: 4.7 litres (8.25 Imp. pints); fuel
tank: 72 litres (16 Imp. gal); cooling system: 17 litres (30 Imp.
pints).
   Notes: Two-door, two-seater, sports coupe. V-8, 220 bhp
engine and various transmissions optionally available.

GENERAL MOTORS (USA)

CADILLAC FLEETWOOD BROUGHAM　　　6966cc

Chassis: separate frame.
Engine: front-mounted, eight-cylinder, V-configuration, ohv, water-cooled, bore 104mm, stroke 103mm, output 180 bhp at 4000 rev/min, torque 44 kgf.m (320 lbf.ft) at 2000 rev/min, compression ratio 8.2:1.
Carburettor: Rochester, single.
Clutch: N.A.
Transmission: 3F1R, automatic.
Final Drive: rear wheels.
Brakes: disc front, drum rear.
Steering: recirculating ball, power assisted.
Suspension: independent coil springs front, coil springs rear.
Tyres: HR 78 x 15.
Dimensions, length: 5615mm (18ft 5in); width: 1935mm (6ft 4.5in); height: 1448mm (4ft 9in); wheelbase: 3086mm (10ft 1.5in).
Capacities, engine sump: 4.7 litres (8.25 Imp. pints); fuel tank: 91 litres (20 Imp. gal); cooling system: 17 litres (30 Imp. pints).
　　Notes: Latest version features new electronic rear suspension levelling system and a number of detail engine modifications.

GINETTA (GB)

G21-1800   **1725cc**

Chassis: tubular frame.
Engine: front-mounted, four-cylinder, in-line, ohv, water-cooled, bore 81.5mm, stroke 82.5mm, output 83 bhp at 5200 rev/min, torque 13.8 kgf.m (100 lbf.ft) at 3800 rev/min, compression ratio: 9.2:1.
Carburettor: Zenith Stromberg twin.
Clutch: diaphragm, sdp.
Transmission: 4F1R, manual a/s, overdrive optional.
Final Drive: rear wheels.
Brakes: disc front, drum rear.
Steering: rack and pinion.
Suspension: independent coil spring front and rear.
Tyres: 165 SR 13.
Dimensions, length: 3975mm (13ft 0.5in); width: 1600mm (5ft 3in); height: 1168mm (3ft 10in); wheelbase: 2311mm (7ft 7in); weight-unladen 785 kg (1730 lb).
Capacities, engine sump: 4.3 litres (7.5 Imp. pints); fuel tank: 45 litres (20 Imp. gal); cooling system: 8 litres (14 Imp. pints).
   Notes: Introduced 1971. Uses Chrysler 1725cc power unit. Also available is the G21-1800S with the Chrysler Holbay engine, twin Weber carburettors and an output of 106 bhp.

HONDA (J)

ACCORD

1600cc

Chassis: unitary construction.
Engine: front transversely-mounted, four-cylinder, in-line, ohc, watercooled, bore 74mm, stroke 93mm, output 79bhp at 5300 rev/min, torque 12.7 kgf.m (91.8 lbf.ft) at 3700 rev/min, compression ratio 8.4:1.
Carburettor: KEIHIN One-twin choke 20/26.
Clutch: diaphragm, sdp.
Transmission: 5F1R, automatic optional.
Final Drive: front wheels.
Brakes: disc front, drum rear.
Steering: rack and pinion.
Suspension: independent MacPherson strut and coil front and rear.
Tyres: 155 x 13.
Dimensions, length: 4125mm (13ft 4.75in); width: 1620mm (5ft 3in); height: 1335mm (4ft 3.6in); wheelbase: 2380mm (7ft 9in); weight: 890 kg (1962.5 lb).
Capacities, engine sump: 3.70 litres (6.5 Imp. pints); fuel tank: 50 litres (11 Imp. gal); cooling system: 5.7 litres (10 Imp. pints).
  Notes: Introduced in the UK 1977. Standard equipment includes maintenance indicators on the instrument panel and a tailgate lock on the Drivers' side door sill.

HONDA (J)

CIVIC 1200   1238cc

Chassis: unitary construction.
Engine: front, transversely-mounted, four-cylinder, in-line, ohc, water-cooled, bore 72mm, stroke 76mm, output 55 bhp at 5500 rev/min, torque 8.6 kgf.m (62.2 lbf.ft) at 3000 rev/min, compression ratio 8.1:1.
Carburettor: KEIHIN twin choke.
Clutch: diaphragm, sdp.
Transmission: 4F1R, manual, a/s Hondamatic optional.
Final Drive: front wheels.
Brakes: disc front, drum rear, servo-assisted.
Steering: rack and pinion.
Suspension: independent, coils front and rear.
Tyres: 155 SR 12.
Dimensions, length: 3545mm (11ft 6.25in); width: 1505mm (4ft 10.75in); height: 1330mm (4ft 3.5in); wheelbase: 2200mm (7ft 1.75in); weight: 790 kg (1742 lb).
Capacities, engine sump: 3 litres (5.25 Imp. pints); fuel tank: 4.75 litres (8.4 Imp. gal); cooling system: 4 litres (7 Imp. pints).
   Notes: Introduced in 1973 with 2-door and 3-door body options. A 1500cc, 4-door version is available at the top of the range.

LADA (SU)

1300 ES   **1294cc**

Chassis: unitary construction.
Engine: front-mounted, four-cylinder, V-configuration, ohc, water-cooled, bore 79mm, stroke 66mm, output 67 bhp at 5600 rev/min, torque 9.5 kgf.m (69 lbf. ft) at 3400 rev/min, compression ratio: 8.5:1.
Carburettor: Russian, single.
Clutch: diaphragm, sdp.
Transmission: 4F1R, manual a/s.
Final Drive: rear wheels.
Brakes: disc front, drum rear.
Steering: worm and roller.
Suspension: independent coil spring front, coil spring rear.
Tyres: 6.15 13.
Dimensions, length: 4064mm (13ft 4in); width: 1600mm (5ft 3.25in); height: 1372mm (4ft 6.5in); wheelbase: 2413mm (7ft 11.5in); weight: 952 kg (2100 lb).
Capacities, engine sump: 3.8 litres (6.7 Imp. pints); fuel tank: 38.6 litres (8.5 Imp. gal); cooling system: 9.6 litres (16.8 Imp. pints).
  Notes: Introduced 1977. Based on the 1200 body shape but distinguishable by contrasting vinyl roof, triple coachline, rear quarter roof panel vent grilles, new-style bumpers, matt black radiator grille and modified rear light clusters. New 1500 and 1500 ES Estates (1452cc, 75 bhp engine) also available, as are the 1200 Saloon and Estate. Models are derived from the Fiat 124.

LAMBORGHINI (I)

URRACO P300

2996cc

Chassis: unitary construction.
Engine: centre-mounted, eight-cylinder, v-configuration, ohc, water-cooled, bore 86mm, stroke 64.5mm, output 250 bhp at 7500 rev/min, torque 27 kgf.m (195 lbf.ft) at 3500 rev/min, compression ratio: 10:1.
Carburettor: Weber, four.
Clutch: sdp.
Transmission: 5F1R, manual a/s.
Final Drive: rear wheels.
Brakes: disc front and rear, servo-assisted.
Steering: rack and pinion.
Suspension: independent coil spring front and rear.
Tyres: front 195-70VR 14, rear 205-70VR 14.
Dimensions, length: 4285mm (13ft 11.25in); width: 1740mm (5ft 9.25in); height: 1160mm (3ft 7.75in); wheelbase: 2450mm (8ft 0.5in); weight-unladen 1300 kg (2816 lb).
Capacities, engine sump: 10 litres (18 Imp. pints); fuel tank: 80 litres (17 Imp. gal); cooling system: 14 litres (25 Imp. pints).

   Notes: Bodywork designed by Bertone. Top speed over 260 km/h (162 mph). Four-seater (2 + 2) offering leather upholstery and air conditioning as options. First Lamborghini to be powered by a V-8 rather than the traditional V-12.

LAMBORGHINI (I)

SILHOUETTE   2996cc

Chassis: unitary construction.
Engine: centre-mounted, eight-cylinder, V-configuration, ohc, water-cooled, bore 86mm, stroke 64.5mm, output 250 bhp at 7500 rev/min, torque 27 kgf.m (195 lbf.ft) at 3500 rev/min, compression ratio: 10:1.
Carburettor: Weber, four.
Clutch: sdp.
Transmission: 5F1R, manual, a/s.
Final Drive: rear wheels.
Brakes: disc front, and rear, servo-assisted.
Steering: rack and pinion.
Suspension: independent coil springs front and rear.
Tyres: front 195/50 VR 15; rear 285/40 VR 15.
Dimensions, length: 4320mm (14ft 0.5in); width: 1880mm (6ft 1.5in); height: 1120mm (3ft 8in); wheelbase: 2450mm (8ft 0.5in); weight-unladen 1200kg (2646 lb).
Capacities, engine sump: 10 litres (18 lmp. pints); fuel tank: 80 litres (18 lmp. gal); cooling system: 14 litres (25 lmp. pints).
  Notes: Bertone designed, two-seater model, mechanically similar to the Urraco P300.

LAMBORGHINI (I)

ESPADA 400GT

3296cc

Chassis: unitary construction.
Engine: front-mounted, twelve-cylinder, V-configuration, ohc, water-cooled, bore 82mm, stroke 62mm, output 350 bhp at 7500 rev/min, torque 40 kgf.m. (290lbf.ft) at 5500 rev/min, compression ratio: 10.7:1.
Carburettor: Weber, six.
Clutch: sdp.
Transmission: 5F1R, manual a/s.
Final Drive: rear wheels.
Brakes: disc front and rear, servo-assisted.
Steering: rack and pinion.
Suspension: independent coil spring front and rear.
Tyres: 215-70VR 15.
Dimensions, length: 4738mm (15ft 6.5in); width: 1860mm (6ft 1.5in); wheelbase: 2650mm (8ft 8.25in); weight-unladen 1635 kg (3605 lb).
Capacities, engine sump: 15 litres (26.5 Imp. pints); fuel tank: 140 litres (30.75 Imp. gal); cooling system: 16 litres (28 Imp. pints).
   Notes: Four-seater coupe designed by Bertone. Leather upholstery, power-windows and air-conditioning fitted as standard. Top speed 250 km/h (155 mph).

LAMBORGHINI (I)

COUNTACH LP400   3929cc

Chassis: tubular frame.
Engine: central-mounted, twelve-cylinder, V-configuration, ohc, water-cooled, bore 82mm, stroke 62mm, output 375 bhp at 8000 rev/min, torque 37 kgf.m. (266 lbf.ft) at 5000 rev/min, compression ratio: 10.5:1.
Carburettor: Weber, six.
Clutch: sdp.
Transmission: 5FIR, manual a/s.
Final Drive: rear wheels.
Brakes: disc front and rear, servo-assisted.
Steering: rack and pinion.
Suspension: independent coil spring front and rear.
Tyres: front 205-70VR 14, rear 215-70VR 14.
Dimensions, length: 4140mm (13ft 7in); width: 1885mm (6ft 2.5in); height: 1095mm (3ft 6in); wheelbase: 2450mm (8ft 0.5in); weight-unladen 1200 kg (2640 lb).
Capacities, engine sump: 17.5 litres (30.5 Imp. pints); fuel tank: 120 litres (26.5 Imp. gal); cooling system: 17 litres (30 Imp. pints).
  Notes: Introduced in 1971. Bodywork designed by Bertone. Top speed over 300 km/h (185 mph); 0-100 km/h (0-60 mph) in 5.4 s; 0-160 km/h (0-100 mph) in 12.8 s. Fuel consumption 14 mpg.

LANCIA (I)

BETA HPE 2000   **1995cc**

Chassis: unitary construction.
Engine: front-mounted, four-cylinder, V-configuration, ohc, water-cooled, bore 84mm, stroke 90mm, output 119 bhp at 5500 rev/min, torque 17.8 kgf.m (129 lbf.ft) at 2800 rev/min, compression ratio: 8.9:1.
Carburettor: Solex or Weber, single.
Clutch: diaphragm, sdp.
Transmission: 5F1R, manual, a/s.
Final Drive: front wheels.
Brakes: disc front and rear, servo-assisted.
Steering: rack and pinion.
Suspension: independent coil springs front and rear.
Tyres: 175/70 SR 14.
Dimensions, length: 4285mm (14ft 1in); width: 1650mm (5ft 4.75in); height: 1308mm (4ft 3.5in); wheelbase: 2540mm (8ft 3.5in); weight: 1060 kg (2337 lb).
Capacities, engine sump: 5 litres (9 Imp. pints); fuel tank: 59 litres (13 Imp. gal); cooling system: 7.5 litres (13.2 Imp. pints).
  Notes: High Performance Estate (3-door) model featuring a twin cam, transversely mounted engine. Sun-roof fitted as standard. Maximum speed 180 km/h (112 mph). Also available is the HPE 1600 powered by a 1585cc, 100 bhp engine.

LANCIA (I)

GAMMA

2484cc

Chassis: unitary construction.
Engine: front-mounted, horizontally-opposed, four-cylinder, ohc, water-cooled, bore 102mm, stroke 76mm, output 140 bhp at 6000 rev/min, torque 21.2 kgf.m (153 lbf.ft) at 3000 rev/min, compression ratio: 9:1.
Carburettor: Weber.
Clutch: sdp.
Transmission: 5F1R, manual a/s, optional 4F1R automatic.
Final Drive: front wheels.
Brakes: disc all round.
Steering: rack and pinion, power-assisted.
Suspension: independent coil springs front and rear.
Tyres: 185/70HR 14.
Dimensions, length: 4580mm (15ft 4in); width: 1730mm (5ft 9in); height: 1410mm (4ft 7.5in); wheelbase: 2670mm (9ft 7in); weight-unladen: 1320 kg (2904 lb).
Capacities, engine sump: 6 litres (11 Imp. pints); fuel tank: 63 litres (14 Imp. gal); cooling system: 9 litres (16 Imp. pints).
    Notes: Introduced 1976. Four-door, four-seater Berlina (Saloon) designed by Pininfarina. Electrically-powered front-door window lifts and many luxury features fitted as standard. Two-door coupé also available.

LANCIA (I)

MONTE CARLO

1995cc

Chassis: unitary construction.
Engine: mid-mounted, four-cylinder, in-line, ohc, water-cooled, bore 84mm, stroke 90mm, output 120 bhp at 6000 rev/min, torque 16.8 kgf.m (122 lbf.ft) at 3500 rev/min, compression ratio: 8.9:1.
Carburettor: Weber, single.
Clutch: sdp.
Transmission: 5F1R, manual a/s.
Final Drive: rear wheels.
Brakes: disc all round, servo-assisted.
Steering: rack and pinion.
Suspension: independent coil springs front and rear.
Tyres: 185/70HR 13.
Dimensions, length: 3813mm (12ft 7in); width: 1696mm (5ft 6.75in); height: 1190mm (3ft 11in); wheelbase: 2226mm (7ft 6.5in); weight-unladen: 1038 kg (2290 lb).
Capacities, engine sump: 6.2 litres (11 Imp. pints); fuel tank: 60 litres (13 Imp. gal); cooling system: 15 litres (25 Imp. pints).
   Notes: Introduced Spring 1976, Mid-engined, wedge-shaped, two-seater sports model. Available in fixed head or convertible form. The name commemorates a hatrick of Lancia outright victories in the world famous rally during the last 25 years.

LEYLAND CARS (GB)

AUSTIN ALLEGRO (2)

1098cc

Chassis: unitary construction.
Engine: front-mounted, four-cylinder, in-line, ohv, water-cooled, bore 64.6mm, stroke 83.7mm, output 45 bhp at 5250 rev/min, torque 7.6 kgf.m (54.8 lbf.ft) at 2900 rev/min, compression ratio 8.5:1.
Carburettor: SU, single.
Clutch: diaphragm, sdp.
Transmission: 4F1R, manual, a/s.
Final Drive: front wheels.
Brakes: disc front, drum rear.
Steering: rack and pinion.
Suspension: independent 'Hydragas' front and rear.
Tyres: 145 x 13.
Dimensions, length: 3852mm (12ft 7.75in); width: 1613mm (5ft 3.25in); height: 1390mm (4ft 6.75in); wheelbase: 2442mm (8ft 0.25in); weight-unladen: 829 kg (1828 lb).
Capacities, engine sump: 5.1 litres (9 Imp. pints); fuel tank: 47.7 litres (10.5 Imp. gal); cooling system: 4.12 litres (7.25 Imp. pints).
   Notes: Introduced 1973. Smallest model in the range which comprises '1100' (1098cc engine), '1300' (1275cc engine), '1500' (1485cc engine) and '1750' (1748cc engine) models.

LEYLAND CARS (GB)

DAIMLER DOUBLE-SIX VANDEN PLAS 5343cc

Chassis: unitary construction.
Engine: front-mounted, twelve-cylinder, V-configuration, ohc, water-cooled bore 90mm, stroke 70mm, output 285 bhp at 5750 rev/min, torque 41 kgf.m (294 lbf.ft) at 3500 rev/min, compression ratio 9.0:1.
Carburettor: N.A. (fuel inj.).
Clutch: N.A.
Transmission: 3F1R, automatic.
Final Drive: rear wheels.
Brakes: disc front, drum rear, servo-assisted.
Steering: rack and pinion, power-assisted.
Suspension: independent coil springs front and rear.
Tyres: 205/70 VR15.
Dimensions, length: 4945mm (16ft 2.75in); width: 1770mm (5ft 9.75in); height: 1375mm (4ft 6in); wheelbase: 2865mm (9ft 4.75in); weight-unladen: 1860 kg (4300 lb).
Capacities: engine sump: 10.8 litres (19 Imp. pints); fuel tank: 91 litres (20 Imp. gal); cooling system: 20.5 litres (36 Imp. pints).
  Notes: Luxury saloon based on the Jaguar XJ 5.3, but with special appointments by Vanden Plas including, electrically operated windows, extensive use of walnut veneer and special hide seats. 4.2 (4235cc, carburettor engine) version also available.

LEYLAND CARS (GB)

JAGUAR XJ 3.4

3442cc

Chassis: unitary construction.
Engine: front-mounted, six-cylinder, in-line, ohc, water-cooled, bore 83mm, stroke 106mm, compression ratio 8.5:1.
Carburettor: SU, two.
Clutch: sdp.
Transmission: 4F1R, manual, a/s; 3F1R automatic optional.
Final Drive: rear wheels.
Brakes: disc front and rear, servo-assisted.
Steering: rack and pinion, power assisted.
Suspension: independent coil springs front, coil springs rear.
Tyres: E 70 VR 15.
Dimensions, length: 4995mm (16ft 2.75in); width: 1770mm (5ft 9.75in); height: 1375mm (4ft 6in); wheelbase: 2865mm (9ft 4.75in). weight: 1748kg (3841lb).
Capacities, engine sump: 8.25 litres (14.5 Imp. pints); fuel tank: 100 litres (20 Imp. gal); cooling system: 18.5 litres (32.5 Imp. pints).

Notes: XJ range first introduced 1972. Latest range, which incorporates a number of detail changes, comprises the 3.4 (shown) 4.2 (4235cc engine) and 5.3 (5343cc V-12 engine) four-door saloons and 4.2C and 5.3C two-door saloons.

LEYLAND CARS (GB)

JAGUAR XJS   5343cc

Chassis: unitary construction.
Engine: front-mounted, twelve-cylinder, V-configuration, ohc, water-cooled, bore 92mm, stroke 106mm, output 285 bhp at 5800 rev/min, torque 40.7 kgf.m (294 lbf.ft) at 3500 rev/min, compression ratio 9.0:1.
Carburettor: N.A. (fuel inj.).
Clutch: diaphragm, sdp.
Transmission: 4F1R, manual, a/s; 3F1R automatic optional.
Final Drive: rear wheels.
Brakes: disc front and rear, servo-assisted.
Steering: rack and pinion, power-assisted.
Suspension: independent coil springs front and rear.
Tyres: 205/ VR 15.
Dimensions, length: 4870mm (15ft 11.75in); width: 1790mm (5ft 10.5in); height: 1260mm (4ft 1.75mm); wheelbase: 2590mm (8ft 6in); weight-unladen: 1687 kg (3710 lb).
Capacities, engine sump: 10.8 litres (19 Imp. pints); fuel tank: 86 litres (19 Imp. gal); cooling system: 20.5 litres (36 Imp. pints).
   Notes: Two-door, four-seater with a top speed of over 250 km/h (150 mph) and capable of 0-100 km/h (0-60 mph) in 6.8 s. Other features include electronic fuel injection, telescopic bumpers, quartz halogen biode headlamps and electrically-operated windows.

LEYLAND CARS (GB)

MAXI HL **1748cc**

Chassis: unitary construction.
Engine: front-mounted, four-cylinder, in-line, ohc, water-cooled, bore 76.2mm, stroke 95.75mm, output 91 bhp at 5250 rev/min, torque 14.38 kgf.m (103.9 lbf.ft) at 3400 rev/min, compression ratio 9.5:1.
Carburettor: SU, two.
Clutch: diaphragm, sdp.
Transmission: 5F1R, manual, a/s.
Final Drive: front wheels.
Brakes: disc front, drum rear, servo-assisted.
Steering: rack and pinion.
Suspension: independent "Hydrolastic" front and rear.
Tyres: 165 13.
Dimensions, length: 4022mm (13ft 2.25in); width: 1629mm (5ft 4.25in); height: 1403mm (4ft 7.25in); wheelbase: 2642mm (8ft 8in); weight-unladen: 1005 kg (2216 lb).
Capacities, fuel tank: 47.7 litres (10.5 Imp. gal).
   Notes: Five-door Maxi. First introduced in 1969 (1750 added in 1970; HL in 1972). The 1500 model is powered by a 1485cc, 68 bhp engine and the 1750 by a 72 bhp version of the 1748cc engine. Fifth gear has an overdrive ratio.

MG MIDGET

1493cc

Chassis: unitary construction.
Engine: front-mounted, four-cylinder, in-line, ohv, water-cooled, bore 73.7mm, stroke 87.5mm, output 65 bhp at 5500 rev/min, torque 10.6 kgf.m (76.5 lbf.ft) at 3000 rev/min, compression ratio 9.0:1.
Carburettor: SU, two.
Clutch: diaphragm, sdp.
Transmission: 4F1R, manual, a/s.
Final Drive: rear wheels.
Brakes: disc front, drum rear.
Steering: rack and pinion.
Suspension: independent coil springs front, leaf springs rear.
Tyres: 145 13.
Dimensions, length: 3580mm (11ft 9in); width: 1530mm (5ft 9.25in); height: 1230mm (4ft 0.25in); wheelbase: 2030mm (6ft 8in); weight-unladen: 805 kg (1774 lb).
Capacities, engine sump: 4 litres (7 Imp. pints); fuel tank: 32 litres (7 Imp. gal); cooling system: 5.75 litres (10 Imp. pints).
   Notes: Introduced 1961 (Mark III 1966). Two-seater sports car featuring a Triumph 1500 TC engine and Morris Marina gearbox. Fitted with polyurethane energy-absorbing bumpers, front and rear.

LEYLAND CARS (GB)

MG MGB

1798cc

Chassis: unitary construction.
Engine: front-mounted, four-cylinder, in-line, ohv, water-cooled, bore 80.25mm, stroke 88.9mm, output 97 bhp at 5500 rev/min, torque 14.5 kgf.m (104.8 lbf.ft) at 2500 rev/min, compression ratio 9.0:1.
Carburettor: SU, two.
Clutch: diaphragm, sdp.
Transmission: 4F1R, manual, a/s.
Final Drive: rear wheels.
Brakes: disc front, drum rear, servo-assisted.
Steering: rack and pinion.
Suspension: independent coil springs front, leaf springs rear.
Tyres: 165 SR 14.
Dimensions, length: 4020mm (13ft 2.25in); width: 1570mm (5ft 1.75in); height: 1300mm (4ft 3in); wheelbase: 2310mm (7ft 7in); weight-unladen: 1065 kg (2348 lb).
Capacities, engine sump: 4 litres (7 Imp. pints); fuel tank: 50 litres (11 Imp. gal); cooling system: 5.7 litres (10 Imp. pints).
   Notes: Introduced 1962. Two seater sports-car continued with minor modifications. Also available is the MGB GT 2 + 2 Coupé. Maximum speed 172 km/h (107 mph). Both fitted with energy-absorbing, front and rear bumpers.

LEYLAND CARS (GB)

MINI 1000   **998cc**

Chassis: unitary construction.
Engine: front-mounted, four-cylinder, in-line, ohv, water-cooled, bore 64.6mm, stroke 76.2mm, output 39 bhp at 4750 rev/min, torque 7.12 kgf.m (52 lbf.ft) at 2000 rev/min, compression ratio: 8.3:1.
Carburettor: SU, single.
Clutch: diaphragm, sdp.
Transmission: 4F1R, manual, a/s.
Final Drive: front wheels.
Brakes: drum front and rear.
Steering: rack and pinion.
Suspension: independent, rubber cones front and rear.
Tyres: 145 SR 10.
Dimensions, length: 3050mm (10ft 0.25in); width: 1400mm (4ft 7in); height: 1350mm (4ft 5in); wheelbase: 2040mm (6ft 8.25in); weight-unladen: 617 kg (1360 lb).
Capacities, engine sump: 4.7 litres (8.5 Imp. pints); fuel tank: 25 litres (5.5 Imp. gal); cooling system: 3.6 litres (6.25 Imp. pints).

   Notes: Mk II Mini introduced in 1967. Also available is the 850 (848cc, 33 bhp engine). Latest versions feature matt black grille and a coachline. Interior improvements include reclining striped seats and fitted carpets.

LEYLAND CARS (GB)

MINI 1275 GT   **1275cc**

Chassis: unitary construction.
Engine: front-mounted, four-cylinder, in-line, ohv, water-cooled, bore 70.6mm, stroke 81.3mm, output 54 bhp at 5250 rev/min, torque 9.2 kgf.m (66.5 lbf.ft) at 2500 rev/min, compression ratio 8.8:1.
Carburettor: SU, single.
Clutch: diaphragm, sdp.
Transmission: 4F1R, manual, a/s.
Final Drive: front wheels.
Brakes: disc front, drum rear, servo-assisted.
Steering: rack and pinion.
Suspension: independent, rubber cones front and rear.
Tyres: 155/65 SR x 310.
Dimensions, length: 3170mm (10ft 4.5in); width: 1410mm (4ft 7.5in); height: 1360mm (4ft 5.5in); wheelbase: 2040mm (6ft 8.25in); weight-unladen: 675 kg (1488 lb).
Capacities, engine sump: 4.8 litres (8.5 Imp. pints); fuel tank: 25 litres (5.5 Imp. gal); cooling system: 3.5 litres (6.25 Imp. pints).
   Notes: Introduced 1969. High performance version of the Mini Clubman distinguishable by side flashes, GT badges and special wheel trims. Clubman saloon and estate model are powered by a 1098cc, 45 bhp engine.

LEYLAND CARS (GB)

MORRIS MARINA 1.3   1275cc

Chassis: unitary construction.
Engine: front-mounted, four-cylinder, in-line, ohv, water-cooled, bore 70.6mm, stroke 81.3mm, output 57 bhp at 5500 rev/min, torque 9.5 kgf.m (68.7 lbf.ft) at 2450 rev/min, compression ratio 8.8:1.
Carburettor: SU, single.
Clutch: diaphragm, sdp.
Transmission: 4F1R, manual, a/s.
Final Drive: rear wheels.
Brakes: disc front, drum rear.
Steering: rack and pinion.
Suspension: independent torsion bars front, leaf springs rear.
Tyres: 145 x 13.
Dimensions, length: 4213mm (13ft 9.75in); width: 1636mm (5ft 4.5in); height: 1405mm (4ft 7.25in); wheelbase: 2438mm (8ft 0in); weight-unladen: 882 kg (1942 lb).
Capacities, engine sump: 4 litres (7 Imp. pints); fuel tank: 52 litres (11.5 Imp. gal); cooling system: 4.2 litres (7.4 Imp. pints).
    Notes: Introduced 1971 (Mk 2 1975). Range comprises 1.3 De Luxe, 1.3 Super (shown), 1.3 Estate; 1.8 Super, Special and 1.8 Estate (powered by a 1798cc, 72 bhp engine); and GT and HL (powered by 1798cc, 85 bhp engine).

LEYLAND CARS (GB)

PRINCESS 2200 HL   2227cc

Chassis: unitary construction.
Engine: front-mounted, six-cylinder, in-line, ohc, water-cooled, bore 76.2mm, stroke 81.3mm, output 110 bhp at 5250 rev/min, torque 17.1 kgf.m (124 lbf.ft) at 3500 rev/min, compression ratio 9.0:1.
Carburettor: SU, two.
Clutch: diaphragm, sdp.
Transmission: 4F1R, manual, a/s; 3F1R automatic optional.
Final Drive: front wheels.
Brakes: disc front, drum rear, servo-assisted.
Steering: rack and pinion, power-assisted.
Suspension: independent "Hydragas" units front and rear.
Tyres: 185/70 SR 14.
Dimensions, length: 4455mm (14ft 7.5in); width: 1730mm (5ft 8in); height: 1409mm (4ft 7.5in); wheelbase: 2673mm (8ft 9.25in); weight-unladen: 1197 kg (2638 lb).
Capacities, engine sump: 7.4 litres (13 Imp. pints); fuel tank: 72.75 litres (16 Imp. gal); cooling system: 9.6 litres (17 Imp. pints).
   Notes: Introduced 1975 (renamed Princess in 1976). Range comprises 1800, 1800 HL (both powered by a 1798cc 82 bhp engine) 2200 HL (shown) and top of the range 2200 HLS.

LEYLAND CARS (GB)

RANGE ROVER 3528cc

Chassis: separate frame.
Engine: front-mounted, eight-cylinder, V-configuration, ohv, water-cooled, bore 88.9mm, stroke 71.1mm, output 132 bhp at 5000 rev/min, torque 25.8 kgf.m (186.5 lbf.ft) at 2500 rev/min, compression ratio: 8.13:1.
Carburettor: Stromberg, twin.
Clutch: diaphragm, sdp.
Transmission: 4F1R, manual, a/s with two-speed transfer box.
Final Drive: all wheels.
Brakes: disc front, drum rear, servo-assisted.
Steering: recirculating ball.
Suspension: coil springs front and rear.
Tyres: 205 x 16.
Dimensions, length: 4470mm (14ft 8in); width: 1780mm (5ft 10in); height: 1780mm (5ft 10in); wheelbase: 2540mm (8ft 4in); weight-unladen: 1724 kg (3800 lb).
Capacities, engine sump: 5.7 litres (10 Imp. pints); fuel tank: 82 litres (18 Imp. gal); cooling system: 11 litres (20 Imp. pints).
  Notes: Introduced 1970. Four-wheel drive model combining saloon car luxury and all purpose, cross country versatility. Features a 'Boge-Hydromat' self-energising ride-level rear suspension unit. Maximum speed 152 km/h (95 mph).

LEYLAND CARS (GB)

ROVER 2600   2597cc

Chassis: unitary construction.
Engine: front-mounted, six-cylinder, in-line, ohc, water-cooled, bore 81mm, stroke 84mm, output 136 bhp at 5000 rev/min, torque 21 kgf.m (152 lbf.ft) at 3750 rev/min, compression ratio: 9.25:1.
Carburettor: SU, twin.
Clutch: diaphragm, sdp.
Transmission: 5F1R, manual, a/s; 3F1R automatic optional.
Final Drive: rear wheels.
Brakes: disc front, drum rear, servo-assisted.
Steering: rack and pinion.
Suspension: independent coil springs front, coil springs rear.
Tyres: 175 HR 14.
Dimensions, length: 4698mm (15ft 5in); width: 1768mm (5ft 9.5in); height: 1382mm (4ft 6.5in); wheelbase: 2815mm (9ft 2.75in); weight-unladen: 1348 kg (2972 lb).
Capacities, engine sump: 7.1 litres (12.5 Imp. pints); fuel tank: 66 litres (14.5 Imp. gal); cooling system: 10.3 litres (18.25 Imp. pints).
  Notes: Introduced 1977. Smaller engined versions ('2300' with 2350cc, 120 bhp power unit also available) of the award winning five-door, Rover 3500. Layout and equipment differ little from the bigger engined model.

LEYLAND CARS (GB)

TRIUMPH TR7   1998cc

Chassis: unitary construction.
Engine: front-mounted, four-cylinder, in-line, ohc, water-cooled, bore 90.3mm, stroke 78mm, output 105 bhp at 5500 rev/min, torque 16.5 kgf.m (119 lbf.ft) at 3500 rev/min, compression ratio: 9.25:1.
Carburettor: SU, twin.
Clutch: diaphragm, sdp.
Transmission: 4F1R, manual, a/s.
Final Drive: rear wheels.
Brakes: disc front, drum rear, servo-assisted.
Steering: rack and pinion.
Suspension: independent coil springs front, coil springs rear.
Tyres: 175/70 SR 13.
Dimensions, length: 4065mm (13ft 4in); width: 1681mm (5ft 2.25in); height: 1268mm (4ft 2in); wheelbase: 2160mm (7ft 1in); weight-unladen: 1000 kg (2205 lb).
Capacities, engine sump: 4.3 litres (7.5 Imp. pints); fuel tank: 55 litres (12 Imp. gal); cooling system: 5.4 litres (9.5 Imp. pints).
  Notes: Introduced 1975. Wedge-shaped, two-seater model, carrying on the tradition of TR sports-cars, which have been in production since the early fifties. Maximum speed 175 km/h (109 mph). Powered by the Dolomite 2-litre, 16-valve engine.

LEYLAND CARS (GB)

TRIUMPH DOLOMITE 1300   1296cc

Chassis: unitary construction.
Engine: front-mounted, four-cylinder, in-line, ohv, water-cooled, bore 73.7mm, stroke 76mm, output 58 bhp at 5500 rev/min, torque 9.4 kgf.m (68 lbf.ft) at 3300 rev/min, compression ratio: 8.5:1.
Carburettor: SU, single.
Clutch: diaphragm, sdp.
Transmission: 4F1R, manual, a/s.
Final Drive: rear wheels.
Brakes: disc front, drum rear, servo-assisted.
Steering: rack and pinion.
Suspension: independent coil springs front, coil springs rear.
Tyres: 155 SR 13.
Dimensions, length: 4122mm (13ft 6.25in); width: 1588mm (5ft 2.5in); height: 1372mm (4ft 6in); wheelbase: 2453mm (8ft 0.5in); weight-unladen: 943 kg (2079 lb).
Capacities, engine sump: 4.2 litres (7.5 Imp. pints); fuel tank: 57 litres (12.5 Imp. gal); cooling system: 4.8 litres (8.5 Imp. pints).
  Notes: Originally the Triumph Toledo it became part of the Dolomite range in 1976. Also available are the Dolomite 1500 and 1500 HL, both powered by a 1493cc engine.

LEYLAND CARS (GB)

SPITFIRE 1500

1493cc

Chassis: separate frame.
Engine: front-mounted, four-cylinder, in-line, ohv, water-cooled, bore 73.7mm, stroke 87.5mm, output 71 bhp at 5500 rev/min, torque 11.3 kgf.m (82 lbf.ft) at 3000 rev/min, compression ratio: 9.0:1.
Carburettor: SU, twin.
Clutch: diaphragm, sdp.
Transmission: 4F1R, manual, a/s.
Final Drive: rear wheels.
Brakes: disc front, drum rear.
Steering: rack and pinion.
Suspension: independent coil springs front, transverse leaf springs rear.
Tyres: 155 SR 13.
Dimensions, length: 3780mm (12ft 4.75in); width: 1488mm (4ft 10.5in); height: 1162mm (3ft 9.75in); wheelbase: 2110mm (6ft 11in); weight-unladen: 791 kg (1745 lb).
Capacities, engine sump: 4.0 litres (7 Imp. pints); fuel tank: 33 litres (7.25 Imp. gal); cooling system: 4.5 litres (8 Imp. pints).
   Note: Original Spitfire introduced in 1962; redesignated 1500 in 1974. Two-seater sports convertible; hard top optional. Latest version has detail modifications including restyled seats, revised steering column and switches and smaller steering wheel.

LEYLAND CARS (GB)

TRIUMPH DOLOMITE SPRINT   1998cc

Chassis: unitary construction.
Engine: front-mounted, four-cylinder, in-line, ohc, water-cooled, bore 90.3mm, stroke 78mm, output 127 bhp at 5700 rev/min, torque 17 kgf.m (122 lbf.ft) at 4500 rev/min, compression ratio: 9.5:1.
Carburettor: SU, twin.
Clutch: diaphragm, sdp.
Transmission: 4F1R, manual, a/s with overdrive; 3F1R automatic optional.
Final Drive: rear wheels.
Brakes: disc front, drum rear, servo-assisted.
Steering: rack and pinion.
Suspension: independent coil springs front, coil springs rear.
Tyres: 175/70 HR 13.
Dimensions, length: 4122mm (13ft 6.25in); width: 1588mm (5ft 2.5in); height: 1372mm (4ft 6in); wheelbase: 2454mm (8ft 0.5in); weight-unladen: 1041 kg (2295 lb).
Capacities, engine sump: 4.5 litres (8 Imp. pints); fuel tank: 57 litres (12.5 Imp. gal); cooling system: 5.4 litres (9.5 Imp. pints).
   Notes: Introduced 1973. Top model in the Dolomite range, it features a 16-valve head engine and has a maximum speed of 183 km/h (114 mph). Similar to the Dolomite 1850 HL model which is powered by an 1854cc engine.

LEYLAND CARS (GB)

VANDEN PLAS 1500

1485cc

Chassis: unitary construction.
Engine: front-mounted, four-cylinder, in-line, ohc, water-cooled, bore 76.2mm, stroke 81.3mm, output 68 bhp at 5500 rev/min, torque 11.1 kgf.m (80 lbf.ft) at 2900 rev/min, compression ratio 9.0:1.
Carburettor: SU, single.
Clutch: diaphragm, sdp.
Transmission: 5F1R, manual a/s; 4F1R automatic optional.
Final Drive: front wheels.
Brakes: disc front, drum rear, servo-assisted.
Steering: rack and pinion.
Suspension: independent "Hydragas" front and rear.
Tyres: 155SR 13.
Dimensions, length: 3918mm (12ft 10.25in); width: 1613mm (5ft 3.5in); height: 1390mm (4ft 6.75in); wheelbase: 2442mm (8ft 0in); weight-unladen: 728 kg (2763 lb).
Capacities, engine sump: 5.5 litres (9.75 Imp. pints); fuel tank: 48 litres (10.5 Imp. gal); cooling system: 6.5 litres (11.5 Imp. pints).
  Notes: Based on the Allegro, this luxury saloon features a sloping radiator grille reminiscent of the Daimler Vanden Plas, special wheel trims, built-in foglamps, tinted glass and luxurious interior including a walnut veneer facia and deep-pile carpeting.

LOTUS (GB)

ECLAT

1973cc

Chassis: separate frame.
Engine: front-mounted, four-cylinder, in-line, ohc, water-cooled, bore 95.2mm stroke 62.9mm, output 160 bhp at 6200 rev/min, torque 19 kgf.m (140 lbf.ft) at 4900 rev/min, compression ratio: 9.5:1.
Carburettor: Dellorto, two.
Clutch: diaphragm, sdp.
Transmission: 4F1R, manual a/s.
Final Drive: rear wheels.
Brakes: disc front, drum rear, servo-assisted.
Steering: rack and pinion, power-assistance optional.
Suspension: independent coil springs front and rear.
Tyres: 185/70HR 13.
Dimensions, length: 4458mm (14ft 7.5in); width: 1816mm (5ft 11.5in); height: 1220mm (3ft 11.75in); wheelbase: 2483mm (8ft 1.75in); weight-unladen 980 kg (2160 lb).
Capacities, engine sump: 6 litres (11 Imp. pints); fuel tank: 67 litres (14.7 Imp. gal); cooling system: 8.5 litres (15 Imp. pints).
    Notes: Successor to the Lotus Elan 2 + 2, this occasional 4-seater sports model is powered by the highly successful 16-valve, 2-litre Lotus 907 engine, has a top speed of 130 mph and includes many safety features and luxury fitments. Available to 520 (shown), 521, 522, 523 or 524 specifications.

LOTUS (GB)

ESPRIT

1973cc

Chassis: separate frame.
Engine: centre-mounted, four-cylinder, in-line, ohc, water-cooled, bore 95.2mm, stroke 69.2mm, output 160 bhp at 6200 rev/min, torque 19 kgf.m (140 lbf.ft) at 4900 rev/min, compression ratio: 9.5:1.
Carburettor: Dellorto, two.
Clutch: diaphragm, sdp.
Transmission: 5F1R, manual a/s.
Final Drive: rear wheels.
Brakes: disc front and rear.
Steering: rack and pinion.
Suspension: independent coil spring front and rear.
Tyres: 195/70HR 14 front, 205/70HR 14 rear.
Dimensions, length: 4220mm (13ft 9in); width: 1830mm (6ft 1.25in); height: 1095mm (3ft 7.75in); wheelbase: 2440mm (8ft 0in); weight-unladen 898 kg (1980 lb).
Capacities, engine sump: 6 litres (11 Imp. pints); fuel tank: 68 litres (15 Imp. gal); cooling system: 8.5 litres (15 Imp. pints).
   Notes: Two-seater car the glass fibre reinforced plastic body and interior of which were designed by Giugiaro. Top speed 225 km/h (138 mph); 0-100 km/h (0-60 mph) in 6.8 s. Specification includes four retractable headlamps and power windows.

LOTUS (GB)

ELITE

1973cc

Chassis: separate frame.
Engine: front-mounted, four-cylinder, in-line, ohc, water-cooled, bore 95.2mm, stroke 69.2mm, output 155 bhp at 6500 rev/min, torque 18.6 kgf.m (135 lbf. ft) at 5000 rev/min, compression ratio: 9.5:1.
Carburettor: Dellorto, two.
Clutch: diaphragm, sdp.
Transmission: 5F1R, manual a/s, automatic transmission optional.
Final Drive: rear wheels.
Brakes: disc front, drum rear, servo-assisted.
Steering: rack and pinion.
Suspension: independent coil springs front and rear.
Tyres: 205/60VR 14.
Dimensions, length: 4490mm (14ft 11.75in); width: 1790mm (5ft 11.5in); height: 1190mm (3ft 11.5in); wheelbase: 2483mm (8ft 1.75in); weight-unladen 1138 kg (2510 lb).
Capacities, engine sump: 6 litres (11 Imp. pints); fuel tank: 68 litres (15 Imp. gal); cooling system: 8.5 litres (5 Imp. pints).
   Notes: Introduced 1974. Available to 501 (shown), 502, 503 or 504 specification. 502 includes air conditioning, tinted glass and stereo radio tape deck, 503 as 502 plus power steering and 504 as 503 plus automatic transmission.

MAZDA (J)

HATCHBACK (323)   1272cc

Chassis: unitary construction.
Engine: front-mounted, four-cylinder, in-line, ohc, water-cooled, bore 73mm, stroke 76mm, output 60 bhp at 5500 rev/min, torque 9.5 kgf.m (69 lbf.ft) at 3500 rev/min, compression ratio: 9.2:1.
Carburettor: Hitachi, single.
Clutch: diaphragm, sdp.
Transmission: 4F1R, manual, a/s; 3F1R automatic optional.
Final Drive: rear wheels.
Brakes: disc front, drum rear, servo-assisted.
Steering: recirculating ball.
Suspension: independent coil springs, front and rear.
Tyres: 155 SR 13.
Dimensions, length: 3820mm (12ft 6in); width: 1595mm (5ft 3in); height: 1375mm (4ft 6in); wheelbase: 2315mm (7ft 7in); weight 845 kg (1863 lb).
Capacities, engine sump: 3 litres (5.25 Imp. pints); fuel tank: 40 litres (8.8. Imp. gal); cooling system: 5.5 litres (9.7 Imp. pints).
   Notes: Introduced 1977 (U.K.). Range comprises the 1000 3-door, 1300 3-door, 1300 Deluxe and, shown, the 1300 5-door DeLuxe. Latest DeLuxe models have a split rear seat back and electrically-operated control for the tail-gate.

MAZDA (J)

818 SERIES   **1272cc**

Chassis: unitary construction.
Engine: front-mounted, four-cylinder, in-line, ohc, water-cooled, bore 73mm, stroke 76mm, output 66 bhp at 6000 rev/min, torque 9.4 kgf.m (68 lbf.ft) at 3500 rev/min, compression ratio: 9.2:1.
Carburettor: Stromberg, single.
Clutch: sdp.
Transmission: 4F1R, manual a/s, 3F1R automatic optional.
Final Drive: rear wheels.
Brakes: front disc, rear drum.
Steering: recirculating ball.
Suspension: front coil springs, rear leaf springs.
Tyres: 155 SR 13.
Dimensions, length: 4095mm (13ft 4in); width: 1595mm (5ft 3in); height: 1405mm (4ft 7in); wheelbase: 2310mm (7ft 7in); weight-unladen 910 kg (1820 lb).
Capacities, engine sump: 3 litres (5.25 Imp. pints); fuel tank: 45 litres (10 Imp. gal); cooling system: 5-6 litres (9.75 Imp. pints).
  Notes: Available as four-door saloon, estate (shown) and two-door coupé. The engine is a more powerful version of the unit powering the Mazda 1300 range.

MAZDA (J)

Chassis: unitary construction.
Engine: front-mounted, four-cylinder, in-line, ohc, water-cooled, bore 78mm, stroke 83mm, output 75 bhp at 5000 rev/min, torque 11.8 kgf.m (85 lbf.ft) at 3500 rev/min, compression ratio: 8.6:1.
Carburettor: Stromberg, single.
Clutch: diaphragm, sdp.
Transmission: 4F1R, manual a/s.
Final Drive: rear wheels.
Brakes: front disc, rear drum, power-assisted.
Steering: recirculating ball.
Suspension: coil springs front and rear.
Tyres: 165SR 13.
Dimensions, length: 4260mm (14ft 0in); width: 1580mm (5ft 2in); height: 1435mm (4ft 8in); wheelbase: 2470mm (8ft 1in); weight-unladen 970 kg (2135 lb).
Capacities, engine sump: 3.6 litres (6.25 Imp. pints); fuel tank: 50 litres (11 Imp. gal); cooling system: 7 litres (12.25 Imp. pints).
   Notes: Four-door saloon. Specification includes heated rear window and reclining front seats.

MAZDA (J)

Chassis: unitary construction.
Engine: front-mounted, four-cylinder, in-line, ohc, water-cooled, bore 80mm, stroke 88mm, output 83 bhp at 5000 rev/min, torque 13.7 kgf.m (98 lbf.ft) at 2500 rev/min, compression ratio: 8.6:1.
Carburettor: down-draught.
Clutch: diaphragm sdp.
Transmission: 4F1R, manual a/s.
Final Drive: rear wheels.
Brakes: disc front, drum rear, power-assisted.
Steering: recirculating ball.
Suspension: independent coil springs front, leaf spring rear.
Tyres: 175SR 13.
Dimensions, length: 4405mm (14ft 3.75in); width: 1660mm (5ft 5in); wheelbase: 2510mm (8ft 3in); weight-unladen 1095 kg (2415 lb).
Capacities, engine sump: 3.6 litres (6.4 Imp. pints); fuel tank: 65 litres (14.3 Imp. gal); cooling system: 7 litres (12.5 Imp. pints).
  Notes: Available as four-door saloon, two-door coupé (shown) and five-door estate.

MERCEDES BENZ (D)

Chassis: unitary construction.
Engine: front-mounted, four-cylinder, in-line, ohc, water-cooled, bore 93.7mm, stroke 83.6mm, output 109 bhp at 4800 rev/min, torque 19 kgf.m (137 lbf.ft) at 3000 rev/min, compression ratio 9.0:1.
Carburettor: Stromberg, single.
Clutch: diaphragm, sdp.
Transmission: 4F1R, automatic; 4F1R manual optional.
Final Drive: rear wheels.
Brakes: disc front, drum rear, servo-assisted.
Steering: recirculating ball, power-assisted.
Suspension: independent coil psrings front, coil springs rear.
Tyres: 175 SR 14.
Dimensions, length: 4725mm (15ft 6in); width: 1786mm (5ft 10.25in); height: 1441mm (4ft 8.75in); wheelbase: 2795mm (9ft 2in); weight: 1350 kg (2978 lb).
Capacities, engine sump: 5 litres (8.75 Imp. pints); fuel tank: 65 litres (14.25 Imp. gal); cooling system: 9.75 litres (17 Imp. pints).

    Notes: Latest version introduced in 1976. Features new-look, longer, body styling of the other medium-sized Mercedes saloons (200, 200D, 240D, 250, 280E, 300D) with integral foglamps giving a four lamp layout (headlamps are round except on the 280E). New coupé and estate models also available.

MERCEDES BENZ (D)

250

2525cc

Chassis: unitary construction.
Engine: front-mounted, six-cylinder, in-line, ohc, water-cooled, bore 86mm, stroke 72.5mm, output 129 bhp at 5500 rev/min, torque 20 kgf.m (144.6 lbf.ft) at 3500 rev/min, compression ratio 8.7:1.
Carburettor: Stromberg, single.
Clutch: N.A.
Transmission: 4F1R, automatic.
Final Drive: rear wheels.
Brakes: discs front and rear, servo-assisted.
Steering: recirculating ball, power-assisted.
Suspension: independent coil springs front, coil springs rear.
Tyres: 175 SR 14.
Dimensions, length: 4725mm (15ft 5.75in); width: 1786mm (5ft 10.25in); height: 1441mm (4ft 8.75in); wheelbase: 2795mm (9ft 2in); weight: unladen 1360 kg (2999 lb).
Capacities, engine sump: 6 litres (10.5 Imp. pints); fuel tank: 65 litres (14.25 imp. gal); cooling system: 10.25 litres (18 Imp. pints).

Notes: Introduced 1977 (U.K.). Latest addition to the recently facelifted medium-sized range, featuring a newly developed 2.5 litre engine. Maximum speed 175 km/h (109 mph).

MERCEDES BENZ (D)

280 SE   **2746cc**

Chassis: unitary construction.
Engine: front-mounted, six-cylinder, in-line, ohc, water-cooled, bore 86mm, stroke 78.8mm, output 177 bhp at 6000 rev/min, torque 23.8 kgf.m (172 lbf.ft) at 4500 rev/min, compression ratio 8.7:1.
Carburettor: N.A. (fuel inj.).
Clutch: N.A.
Transmission: 4F1R, automatic; 4F1R manual, a/s optional.
Final Drive: rear wheels.
Brakes: discs front and rear, servo-assisted.
Steering: recirculating ball, power-assisted.
Suspension: independent coil springs front, coil springs rear.
Tyres: 185 HR 14.
Dimensions, length: 4960mm (16ft 1¼in); width: 1870mm (6ft 1.5in); height: 1425mm (4ft 8in); wheelbase: 2865mm (9ft 4.75in); weight-unladen: 1610 kg (3550 lb).
Capacities, engine sump: 6 litres (10.5 Imp. pints); fuel tank: 96 litres (21 Imp. gal); cooling system: 11 litres (19.5 Imp. pints).
   Notes: Smallest model in the "S-class", the 280SE ("Super Einspritzmotor") has a top speed of 193 km/h (121 mph). 350 SE has same bodywork and similar trim but is powered by a 3499cc, 195 bhp, V-8, engine with 3-speed automatic transmission.

MERCEDES BENZ (D)

280 CE **2746cc**

Chassis: unitary construction.
Engine: front-mounted, six-cylinder, in-line, ohc, water-cooled, bore 86mm, stroke 78.8mm, output 177 bhp at 6000 rev/min, torque 23.8 kgf.m (166 lbf.ft) at 4500 rev/min, compression ratio 8.7:1.
Carburettor: N.A. (fuel inj.).
Clutch: N.A.
Transmission: 4F1R, automatic; 4F1R manual, a/s optional.
Final Drive: rear wheels.
Brakes: disc front and rear, servo-assisted.
Steering: recirculating ball power-assisted.
Suspension: independent coil springs front and rear.
Tyres: 195/70 HR 14.
Dimensions, length: 4640mm (15ft 2.75in); width: 1786mm (5ft 10.25in); height: 1395mm (4ft 7in); wheelbase: 2710mm (8ft 10.75in); weight-unladen: 1450 kg (3197 lb).
Capacities, engine sump: 6 litres (10.5 Imp. pints); fuel tank: 80 litres (17.5 Imp. gall); cooling system: 10 litres (17.5 Imp. pints).
   Notes: Introduced 1977. Based on the medium-sized saloon range, this new coupé is both lower and shorter. Available as 230C (2307cc, 109 bhp engine), 280C (2746cc, 156 bhp engine) — not in U.K. — and 280CE (shown). Has the same headlamp layout as the 280E saloon.

MERCEDES BENZ (D)

300 D   **3005cc**

Chassis: unitary construction.
Engine: front-mounted, five-cylinder, in-line, water-cooled, bore 91mm, stroke 92.4mm, output 80 bhp at 4000 rev/min, torque 17.5 kgf.m (126.5 lbf.ft) at 2400 rev/min, compression ratio 21:1.
Carburettor: N.A. (fuel inj.).
Clutch: N.A.
Transmission: 4F1R, automatic.
Final Drive: rear wheels.
Brakes: disc front and rear, servo-assisted.
Steering: recirculating ball, power-assisted.
Suspension: independent coil springs.
Tyres: 175 SR 14.
Dimensions, length: 4725mm (15ft 6in); width: 1786mm (5ft 10.25in); height: 1441mm (4ft 8.75in); wheelbase: 2795mm (9ft 2in); weight: 1445 kg (3186 lb).
Capacities, fuel tank: 65 litres (14.3 Imp. gal).
  Notes: Introduced 1976. Only five-cylinder series produced — diesel-engined car in the world. Maximum speed 143 km/h (90 mph). Other diesel models are the 200D (1988cc, 4 cyl. engine) and 240D (2404cc, 4 cyl. engine).

MERCEDES BENZ (D)

350 SL   **3499cc**

Chassis: unitary construction.
Engine: front-mounted, eight-cylinder, V-configuration, ohc, water-cooled, bore 92mm, stroke 65.8mm, output 200 bhp at 5800 rev/min, torque 29.2 kgf.m (211 lbf.ft) at 4000 rev/min, compression ratio 9.5:1.
Carburettor: N.A. (fuel inj.).
Clutch: diaphragm, sdp.
Transmission: 4F1R, manual, a/s; 4F1R automatic optional.
Final Drive: rear wheels.
Brakes: discs front and rear, servo-assisted.
Steering: recirculating ball, power-assisted.
Suspension: independent coil springs front and rear.
Tyres: 205/70 VR 14.
Dimensions: length: 4390mm (14ft 4.75in); width: 1790mm (5ft 10.5in); height: 1300mm (4ft 3.25in); wheelbase: 2460mm (8ft 0.75in); weight-unladen: 1543 kg (3405 lb).
Capacities: engine sump: 7.5 litres (13.25 Imp. pints); fuel tank: 90 litres (19.75 Imp. gal); cooling system: 14.25 litres (25 Imp. pints).
  Notes: Introduced 1971. Maximum speed 202 km/h (126 mph). 450 SL (introduced 1973) has the same bodywork but is powered by a V-8, 4502cc, 225 bhp engine and mechanically similar to the 450 SLC, which is longer and slightly heavier.

MERCEDES BENZ (D)

450 SEL 6.9

6834cc

Chassis: unitary construction.
Engine: front-mounted, eight-cylinder, V-configuration, ohc, water-cooled, bore 107mm, stroke 95mm, output 286 bhp at 4250 rev/min, torque 56 kgf.m (390 lbf.ft) at 3000 rev/min, compression ratio 8.8:1.
Carburettor. N.A. (fuel inj.).
Clutch: N.A.
Transmission: 3F1R, automatic.
Final Drive: rear wheels.
Brakes: disc front and rear, servo-assisted.
Steering: recirculating ball, power assisted.
Suspension: independent, hydropneumatic front and rear.
Tyres: 215/70 VR 14.
Dimensions, length: 5060mm (16ft 7.25in); width: 1860mm (6ft 1.25in); height: 1420mm (4ft 8in); wheelbase: 2960mm (9ft 8.5in); weight: 1935 kg (4265 lb).
Capacities, engine sump: 12 litres (21 Imp. pints); fuel tank: 96 litres (21 Imp. gal); cooling system: 16 litres (28.25 Imp. pints).
   Notes: Introduced 1977 (U.K.). Latest and most powerful addition to "S-class" range. Wider tyres and a 6.9 boot badge are the only external indications that this model differs from the 4.5 litre engined 450 SEL. Features a limited slip differential and air conditioning.

MORGAN (GB)

Chassis: separate frame.
Engine: front-mounted, four-cylinder, in-line, ohv, water-cooled, bore 81mm, stroke 77.62mm, output 84 bhp at 5500 rev/min, torque 12.7 kgf.m (92 lbf.ft) at 3500 rev/min, compression ratio: 9:1.
Carburettor: Weber, single.
Clutch: diaphragm, sdp.
Transmission: 4F1R, manual a/s.
Final Drive: rear wheels.
Brakes: disc front, drum rear.
Steering: worm and nut.
Suspension: independent coil spring front, leaf spring rear.
Tyres: 165 15.
Dimensions, length: 3660mm (12ft 0in); width: 1420mm (4ft 8in); height: 1290mm (4ft 3in); wheelbase: 2440mm (8ft 0in); weight-unladen 735 kg (1624 lb).
Capacities, engine sump: 4 litres (7 Imp. pints); fuel tank: 39 litres (8.5 Imp. gal); cooling system: 7 litres (12.5 Imp. pints).
   Notes: Two-seater sports saloon. Also available as four-seater, Centre lock wire wheels are optional equipment. Top speed over 160 km/h (100 mph). Four-seater has 45.5 litre (10 gal.) fuel tank.

MORGAN (GB)

PLUS 8   **3528cc**

Chassis: separate frame.
Engine: front-mounted, eight-cylinder, V-configuration, ohv, water-cooled, bore 89mm, stroke 71mm, output 155 bhp at 5250 rev/min, torque 27.5 kgf.m (198 lbf.ft) at 2500 rev/min, compression ratio: 9.5:1.
Carburettor: SU, twin.
Clutch: diaphragm, sdp.
Transmission: 5F1R, manual a/s.
Final Drive: rear wheels.
Brakes: disc front, drum rear, servo-assisted.
Steering: worm and nut.
Suspension: front independent coil springs, rear leaf springs.
Tyres: 195 14.
Dimensions, length: 3730mm (12ft 3in); width: 1580mm (5ft 2in); height: 1320mm (4ft 4in); wheelbase: 2490mm (8ft 1in); weight-unladen 828 kg (1826 lb).
Capacities, engine sump: 5.7 litres (10 Imp. pints); fuel tank: 61 litres (13.5 Imp. gal); cooling system: 9.1 litres (16 Imp. pints).
   Notes: Introduced 1968. Maximum speed 200 km/h (125 mph) approx. Rover V-8 engine and gearbox. Distinctive wheels provide easy identification.

OPEL (D)

KADETT CITY SPECIAL

1196cc

Chassis: unitary construction.
Engine: front-mounted, four-cylinder, in-line, ohv, water-cooled, bore 79mm, stroke 61mm, output 52 bhp at 5600 rev/min, torque 8.5 kgf.m (56 lbf.ft) at 3400 rev/min, compression ratio: 7.8:1.
Carburettor: Solex, single.
Clutch: diaphragm, sdp.
Transmission: 4F1R, manual a/s, 3F1R automatic optional.
Final Drive: rear wheels.
Brakes: disc front, drum rear, servo-assisted.
Steering: rack and pinion.
Suspension: independent coil spring front, coil spring rear.
Tyres: 155SR 13.
Dimensions, length: 3890mm (12ft 9.25in); width: 1580mm (5ft 2.25in); Height: 1405mm (4ft 6.25in); wheelbase: 2420mm (7ft 0.25in); weight-unladen: 795 kg (1752 lb).
Capacities, engine sump: 2.8 litres (4.75 Imp. pints); fuel tank: 45 litres (9.75 Imp. gal); cooling system: 4.5 litres (8 Imp. pints).
   Notes: Three-door model — City Luxus version also available — with choice of three engines (1.0 litre and 1.2 litre S optional). Latest addition (1976) to Kadett range which includes the Special two- and four-door saloons, the coupé and the GT/E.

OPEL (D)

MANTA SR

1897cc

Chassis: unitary construction.
Engine: front-mounted, four-cylinder, in-line, ohv, water-cooled, bore 93mm, stroke 69.8mm, output 90 bhp at 4800 rev/min, torque 15 kgf.m (108 lbf.ft) at 3800 rev/min, compression ratio: 8.8:1.
Carburettor: Zenith, single.
Clutch: diaphragm, sdp.
Transmission: 4F1R, manual a/s 3F1R automatic optional.
Final Drive: rear wheels.
Brakes: disc front, drum rear, servo-assisted.
Steering: rack and pinion.
Suspension: independent coil springs front, coil springs rear.
Tyres: 185/70SR 13.
Dimensions, length: 4470mm (14ft 8.75in); width: 1645mm (5ft 4.75in) height: 1335mm (4ft 4.5in); wheelbase: 2515mm (8ft 3in); weight-unladen: 1000 kg (2204 lb).
Capacities, engine sump: 3.7 litres (6.75 Imp. pints); fuel tank: 50 litres (11 Imp. gal); cooling system: 6.5 litres (11.5 Imp. pints).
   Notes: Introduced 1972. Top model in the Manta range which also includes the 1.6 litre deluxe and 1.9 litre SR.

OPEL (D)

ASCONA 19SR BERLINA   1897cc

Chassis: unitary construction.
Engine: front-mounted, four-cylinder, in-line, ohv, water-cooled, bore 93mm, stroke 69.8mm, output 90 bhp at 4800 rev/min, torque 15 kgf.m (108 lbf.ft) at 3800 rev/min, compression ratio: 8.8:1.
Carburettor: Zenith, single.
Clutch: diaphragm, sdp.
Transmission: 4F1R, manual a/s, 3F1R automatic optional.
Final Drive: rear wheels.
Brakes: disc front, drum rear, servo-assisted.
Steering: rack and pinion.
Suspension: independent coil spring front, coil spring rear.
Tyres: 185/70SR 13.
Dimensions, length: 4320mm (14ft 2in); width: 1650mm (5ft 5in); height: 1405mm (4ft 6.25in); wheelbase: 2515mm (8ft 3in); Weight-unladen: 1000 kg (2205 lb).
Capacities, engine sump: 3.7 litres (6.75 Imp. pints); fuel tank: 50 litres (11 Imp. gal); cooling system: 6.5 litres (11.5 Imp. pints).
   Notes: Introduced 1971 (facelifted version 1976). Top model in the Ascona range. Also available are the standard (1.6 litre) and deluxe (1.6 litre S), two and four-door saloons and 19SR two-door saloon.

OPEL (D)

REKORD   **1897 cc**

Chassis: unitary construction.
Engine: front-mounted, four-cylinder, in-line, ohv, water-cooled, bore 93mm, stroke 69.8mm, output 75 bhp at 4800 rev/min, torque 13.5 kgf.m (98 lbf.ft) at 3400 rev/min, compression ratio: 7.9:1.
Carburettor: Solex, single.
Clutch: diaphragm, sdp.
Transmission: 4F1R, manual a/s; 3F1R automatic optional.
Final Drive: rear wheels.
Brakes: disc front, drum rear, servo-assisted.
Steering: recirculating ball.
Suspension: independent coil spring front, coil springs rear.
Tyres: 175SR 14.
Dimensions, length: 4597mm (15ft 1in); width: 1727mm (5ft 8in); height: 1422mm (4ft 8in); wheelbase: 2667mm (8ft 9in); weight: 1120 kg (2469 lb).
Capacities, engine sump: 3.8 litres (6.75 Imp. pints); fuel tank: 63.6 litres (14 Imp. gal); cooling system: 6.2 litres (11 Imp. pints).
   Notes: latest restyled range available, in L.H. drive form, as two- or four-door saloon (standard, deLuxe, Berlina and 'S') and three- or five-door estate (standard and deluxe). 1.9 litre N engine is standrd (new 2 litre in 90, 100 and 110 bhp form, an economy 1.7 litre engine optional). A 2.1 litre diesel power unit is also available.

OPEL (D)

COMMODORE GS/E 2784cc

Chassis: unitary construction.
Engine: front-mounted, six-cylinder, in-line, ohv, water-cooled, bore 92mm, stroke 69.8mm, output 160 bhp at 5400 rev/min, compression ratio: 9.5:1.
Carburettor: N.A. (fuel injection).
Clutch: diaphragm, sdp.
Transmission: 3F1R, automatic (optional on coupé).
Final Drive: rear wheels.
Brakes: disc front and rear, servo-assisted.
Steering: recirculating ball, power assisted.
Suspension: independent coil spring front, coil spring rear.
Tyres: 195/70 HR 14.
Dimensions, length: 4597mm (15ft 1.25in); width: 1727mm (5ft 8in); height: 1397mm (4ft 7.25in); wheelbase: 2667mm (8ft 9in); weight 1265 kg (2789 lb).
Capacities, engine sump: 5.5 litres (9.7 Imp. pints); fuel tank: 70 litres (15.4 Imp. gal); cooling system: 8.1 litres (14.24 Imp. pints).
   Notes: Latest Commodore range comprises GS 2.8 Saloon (142 bhp, carburettor engine), GS/E 4-door Saloon (shown) and GS/E Coupé (fitted with manual transmission). Maximum speed of GS/E Saloon 186 km/h (118 mph).

PANTHER (GB)

LIMA

2279cc

Chassis: separate frame.
Engine: front-mounted, four-cylinder, in-line, ohc, water-cooled, bore 97.5mm, stroke 76.2mm, output 108 bhp at 5000 rev/min, torque 19 kgf.m (138 lbf.ft) at 3000 rev/min, compression ratio: 8.5:1.
Carburettor: Stromberg, twin.
Clutch: sdp.
Transmission: 4F1R, manual a/s, 3F1R automatic optional.
Final Drive: rear wheels.
Brakes: disc front, drum rear, servo-assisted.
Steering: rack and pinion.
Suspension: independent coil spring front, coil spring rear.
Tyres: 175/70 HR 13.
Dimensions, length: 3607mm (11ft 10in); width: 1620mm (5ft 3.5in); height: 1219mm (4ft 0in); wheelbase: 2461mm (8ft 1in); weight-unladen 816 kg (1800 lb).
Capacities, engine sump: 4.8 litres (8.5 Imp. pints); fuel tank: 45 litres (10 Imp. gal); cooling system: 7.4 litres (13 Imp. pints).
   Notes: Introduced October 1976. Maximum speed 125 mph plus. Features a moulded glass fibre body with steel doors. Uses Vauxhall Magnum engine, drive-line and other mechanical components from Vauxhall. A five-speed ZF gearbox is also optionally available.

PANTHER (GB)

Chassis: separate frame.
Engine: front-mounted, six-cylinder, in-line, ohc, water-cooled, bore 92.07mm, stroke 106mm, output 190 bhp at 5000 rev/min, torque 27.6 kgf.m (200 lbf.ft) at 2000 rev/min, compression ratio: 8:1.
Carburettor: SU, two.
Clutch: diaphragm, sdp.
Transmission: 4F1R, manual a/s, automatic optional.
Final Drive: rear wheels.
Brakes: disc front and rear, servo-assisted.
Steering: rack and pinion.
Suspension: independent coil spring front and rear.
Tyres: 225/70VR 15.
Dimensions, length: 4190mm (13 ft 9in); width: 1740mm (5ft 8.5in); height: 1240mm (4ft 1in); wheelbase: 2820mm (9ft 3in); weight-unladen 1134 kg (2500 lb).
Capacities, engine sump: 7.4 litres (13 Imp. pints); fuel tank: 118 litres (26 Imp. gal); cooling system: 11.5 litres (20 Imp. pints).
    Notes: Luxury model incorporating many options including air-conditioning. Powered by a Jaguar 6 cylinder, 4.2 litre engine.

PANTHER (GB)

DE VILLE SALOON
5343cc

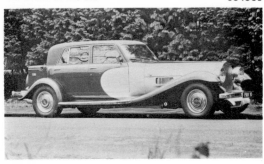

Chassis: separate frame.
Engine: front-mounted, twelve-cylinder, v-configuration, ohc, water-cooled, bore 90mm, stroke 70mm, output 266 bhp at 5750 rev/min, compression ratio: 9:1.
Carburettor: N.A. (fuel injection).
Transmission: 3F1R, automatic standard, 4F1R manual a/s, optional.
Final Drive: rear wheels.
Brakes: disc front and rear, servo-assisted.
Steering: rack and pinion, power assisted.
Suspension: independent coil springs, front and rear.
Tyres: 235/70 HR 15.
Dimensions, length: 5182mm (17ft 0in); width: 1803mm (5ft 11in); height: 1550mm (5ft 1in); wheelbase: 3610mm (11ft 10in); weight-unladen 1973 kg (4360 lb).
Capacities, engine sump: 9.1 litres (16 Imp. pints); fuel tank: 9 litres (22 Imp. gal); cooling system: 20.5 litres (36 Imp. pints).

Notes: Introduced in 1974. Powered by the Jaguar V-12 engine and featuring many XJ 12 mechanical parts. Jaguar 4.2 litre engine also available. The convertible version has an electrically-operated top.

PANTHER (GB)

Chassis: unitary construction with separate front sub-structure.
Engine: centre-mounted, eight-cylinder, V-configuration, ohv, water-cooled, bore 109.2mm, stroke 109.2mm, output 600 bhp at 5500 rev/min, torque 83 kgf.m. (600 lbf.ft), compression ratio 8.5:1.
Carburettor: Holley single.
Clutch: N.A.
Transmission: 3F1R, automatic.
Final Drive: rear wheels.
Brakes: discs front and rear.
Steering: rack and pinion, power-assisted.
Suspension: independent coil springs front and rear.
Tyres: 205/40VR13 front (four); 265/50 VR16 rear
Dimensions: length: 4870mm (16ft 0in); width: 2030mm (6ft 8in); height: 1220mm (4ft 0in); wheelbase: 2670mm (8ft 9in); weight: 1302 kg (2870 lb).
Capacities, engine sump: 5.65 litres (10 Imp. pints); fuel tank: 136.4 litres (30 Imp. gal); cooling system: 24.5 litres (43.2 Imp. pints).

Notes: Introduced 1977. Claimed to be the world's fastest production car, this prestige model features six wheels, a twin-turbocharged 8.2 litre Cadillac V8 engine, Turbo-Hydramatic 425 automatic transmission and a lavish equipment specification which includes detachable hardtop and convertible soft top, air conditioning, electronic instrumentation, automatic fire-extinguishing system, electrically-adjusted seating and windows, push button telephone and television. Maximum speed 320 km/h (200 mph) plus.

PEUGEOT (F)

104 SL   **1124cc**

Chassis: unitary construction.
Engine: front-mounted, four-cylinder, in-line, ohc, water-cooled, bore 72mm, stroke 69mm, output 57 bhp at 6000 rev/min, torque 8.2 kgf.m (59 lbf.ft) at 3000 rev/min, compression ratio: 9.2:1.
Carburettor: Solex, single.
Clutch: diaphragm, sdp.
Transmission: 4F1R, manual, a/s.
Final Drive: front wheels.
Brakes: disc front, drum rear.
Steering: rack and pinion.
Suspension: independent coil springs front and rear.
Tyres: 145 SR/13.
Dimensions, length: 3607mm (11ft 10.25in); width: 1525mm (5ft 0in); height: 1397mm (4ft 7.25in); wheelbase: 2413mm (7ft 11.25in); weight-unladen: 814 kg (1795 lb).
Capacities, engine sump: 4.5 litres (7.9 Imp. pints); fuel tank: 40 litres (8.8 Imp. gal); cooling system: 5.6 litres (9.8 Imp. pints).
   Notes: One of the 104 range first introduced in 1972. Also available are the 104 GL (2-door saloon with 954cc engine) and 104ZS (2-door coupé with 1124cc engine).

PEUGEOT (F)

304 GL   **1290cc**

Chassis: unitary construction.
Engine: front-mounted, four-cylinder, in-line, ohc, water-cooled, bore 78mm, stroke 67.5mm, output 65 bhp at 6000 rev/min, torque 9.6 kgf.m (69 lbf.ft) at 3750 rev/min, compression ratio: 8.8:1.
Carburettor: Solex, single.
Clutch: daiphragm, sdp.
Transmission: 4F1R, manual, a/s.
Final Drive: front wheels.
Brakes: disc front, drum rear, servo-assisted.
Steering: rack and pinion.
Suspension: independent coil springs front and rear.
Tyres: 145 SR/14.
Dimensions, length: 4140mm (13ft 7in); width: 1575mm (5ft 2in); height: 1397mm (4ft 7.5in); wheelbase: 2595mm (8ft 6in); weight-unladen: 930 kg (2050 lb).
Capacities, engine sump: 4 litres (7 Imp. pints); fuel tank: 42 litres (9.25 Imp. gal); cooling system: 5.8 litres (10.25 Imp. pints).
  Notes: Introduced 1969. Also available are the SL Estate (1290cc, 65 bhp engine) GL Estate (1127cc, 59 bhp engine) and SLS (1290cc, 74.5 bhp engine.)

PEUGEOT (F)

504 L   **1796cc**

Chassis: unitary construction:
Engine: front-mounted, four-cylinder, in-line, ohv, water-cooled, bore 84mm, stroke 81mm, output 79 bhp at 5100 rev/min, torque 14.5 kgf.m (104.8 lbf.ft) at 2600 rev/min, compression ratio: 7.5:1.
Carburettor: Solex, single.
Clutch: diaphragm, sdp.
Transmission: 4F1R, manual, a/s.
Final Drive: rear wheels.
Brakes: disc front, drum rear, servo-assisted.
Steering: rack and pinion.
Suspension: independent coil springs front, coil springs rear.
Tyres: 165 SR/14.
Dimensions: length: 4470mm (14ft 8.5in); width: 1676mm (5ft 6.5in); height: 1676mm (5ft 6.5in); wheelbase: 2743mm (9ft 0in); weight-unladen: 1158 kg (2552 lb).
Capacities: engine sump: 4 litres (7 Imp. pints); fuel tank: 56 litres (12.3 Imp. gal); cooling system: 7.8 litres (13.7 Imp. pints).
   Notes: Introduced 1971 (UK). Also available are the 504L Estate, 504 GL (1971cc, 96 bhp engined) Saloon, Estate and Family Estate, 504 TI (1971cc, 106 bhp fuel injection engined) Saloon, 504 L (1948cc, 56 bhp diesel engined) Saloon, 504 L (2112cc, 59 bhp diesel engined) Estate and 504 GL (2304cc, 70 bhp diesel engined) Saloon and Family Estate.

PEUGEOT (F)

Chassis: unitary construction.
Engine: front-mounted, six-cylinder, V-configuration, ohc, water-cooled, bore 88mm, stroke 73mm, output 136 bhp at 5750 rev/min, torque 21.1 kgf.m (152.5 lbf.ft) at 3500 rev/min, compression ratio: 8.65:1.
Carburettor: Solex, single.
Clutch: diaphragm, sdp.
Transmission: 4F1R, manual, a/s; automatic (optional).
Final Drive: rear wheels.
Brakes: disc front and rear, servo-assisted.
Steering: rack and pinion, power-assisted.
Suspension: independent coil springs front, coil springs rear.
Tyres: 175 HR 14.
Dimensions, length: 4724mm (15ft 6in); width: 1778mm (5ft 9.75in); height: 1422mm (4ft 8.25in); wheelbase: 2794mm (9ft 2.25in); weight-unladen: 1455 kg (3208 lb).
Capacities, engine sump: 6 litres (10.5 Imp. pints); fuel tank: 70 litres (15.4 Imp. gal); cooling system: 10.2 litres (17.9 Imp. pints).

   Notes: Introduced 1975. Top of the Peugeot model range powered by a V-6 engine and featuring many luxury fittings including electric windows and sun-roof. Air conditioning is available with the automatic transmission version.

PEUGEOT (F)

305 GL　　　　　　　　　　　　　　　　　　**1290cc**

Chassis: unitary construction.
Engine: transversely-mounted, four-cylinder, in-line, ohv, water-cooled, bore 78mm, stroke 67.5mm, output 65 bhp at 6000 rev/min, torque 9.6 kgf.m at 3750 rev/min, compression ratio 8.8:1.
Carburettor: Solex 34 PBISA5.
Clutch: diaphragm, sdp.
Transmission: 4F1R, manual a/s.
Final Drive: front wheels.
Brakes: disc front, drum rear.
Steering: rack with cardan jointed column.
Suspension: independent coil with MacPherson Struts front, coils rear.
Tyres: 145SR 14.

Dimensions, length: 4237mm (13ft 9.25in); width: 1630mm (5ft 3.5in); height: 1405mm (4ft 6.75in); wheelbase: 2620mm (8ft 6in); weight 925 kg (2040 lb).
Capacities, engine sump: 4 litres (7 Imp. pints); fuel tank: 43 litres (9.5 Imp. gal); cooling system: 5.8 litres (10.2 Imp. pints).
　Notes: Introduced Spring 1978. Also available in the range: 305 GR with more luxurious interior specification, 305 SR fitted with a 1472cc engine and at the top of the range the 1500 SR which includes metal sun roof, tinted glass and electrically operated front windows. The body design has been dirctly derived from the Peugeot SSV (Safety Synthesis Vehicle).

POLSKI-FIAT (PL)

125P   **1481cc**

Chassis: unitary construction.
Engine: front-mounted, four-cylinder, in-line, ohv, water-cooled, bore 77mm, stroke 79.5mm output 75 bhp at 5400 rev/min, torque 12 kgf.m (83 lbf.ft) at 3200 rev/min, compression ratio: 9:1.
Carburettor: Webber, single.
Clutch: sdp.
Transmission: 4F1R, manual a/s.
Final Drive: rear wheels.
Brakes: disc front and rear, servo-assisted.
Steering: worm and roller.
Suspension: independent coil spring front, leaf spring rear.
Tyres: 165 13 radial.
Dimensions, length: 4230mm (13ft 10.5in); width: 1620mm (5ft 4in); height: 1440mm (4ft 8.75in); wheelbase: 2500mm (8ft 3in); weight unladen 1020 kg (2249 lb).
Capacities, engine sump: 3.5 litres (6.2 Imp. pints); fuel tank: 45 litres (10 Imp. gal); cooling system: 7 litres (12 Imp. pints).

   Notes: Basic design is similar to the Fiat 125. Available in both saloon and estate car versions. Like other Eastern bloc nations Poland has imported Western automobile technology in order to develop its own motor industry. Fiat has played a leading role in several such enterprises.

PORSCHE (D)

924 **1984**cc

Chassis: unitary construction.
Engine: front-mounted, four-cylinder, in-line, ohv, water-cooled, bore 86.5mm, stroke 84.4mm, output 125 bhp at 5800 rev/min, torque 16.8 kgf.m. (121.5 lbf.ft) at 3500 rev/min, compression ratio: 9.3:1.
Carburettor: N.A. (fuel inj.).
Clutch: sdp.
Transmission: 3F1R, manual, a/s; 3F1R automatic optional.
Final Drive: rear wheels.
Brakes: disc front, drum rear, servo-assisted.
Steering: rack and pinion.
Suspension: independent coil springs front, independent torsion bars rear.
Tyres: 165HR 14.
Dimensions, length: 4213mm (13ft 8.25in); width: 1685mm (5ft 5.25in); height: 1270mm (4ft 1.5in); wheelbase: 2400mm (7ft 8.75in); weight-unladen: 1080 kg (2381 lb).
Capacities, engine sump: 5 litres (8.75 Imp. pints); fuel tank: 62 litres (13.5 Imp. gal).
   Notes: Introduced Spring 1977 (UK). New hatchback sports car. Latest version incorporates various modifications including front and rear anti-roll bars, high intensity rear fog lamps, pile carpeting and cloth seating material throughout. Also available is the 924 Lux, which is distinguishable from the 924 by wider alloy wheels, tinted glass, rear window wiper and headlamp washers.

PORSCHE (D)

911SC

2994cc

Chassis: unitary construction.
Engine: rear-mounted, six-cylinder, horizontally-opposed, ohv, air-cooled, bore 95mm, stroke 70.4mm, output 180 bhp at 6000 rev/min, compression ratio: 8.5:1.
Carburettor: N.A. (fuel inj.).
Clutch: sdp.
Transmission: 5F1R, manual, a/s.
Final Drive: rear wheels.
Brakes: disc front and rear, servo-assisted.
Steering: rack and pinion.
Suspension: independent torsion bars front and rear.
Tyres: 185/70VR 15.
Dimensions, length: 4290mm (14ft 1in); width: 1613mm (5ft 3.5in); height: 1320mm (4ft 4in); wheelbase: 2273mm (7ft 5.5in); weight-unladen: 1080 kg (2400 lb).
Capacities, engine sump: 17 litres (10 Imp. pints); fuel tank: 80 litres (17.6 Imp. gal).
   Notes: Introduced 1977 to replace the 2.7 litre engined 911 Lux and Carrera 3 models. Maximum speed 224 km/h (140 mph). Sports versions also available.

KITTEN

850cc

Chassis: separate frame.
Engine: front-mounted, four-cylinder, in-line, ohv, water-cooled, bore 62.5mm, stroke 69.09mm, output 40 bhp at 5500 rev/min, torque 6.3 kgf.m (46 lbf.ft) at 3500 rev/min, compression ratio: 9.5:1.
Carburettor: SU, single.
Clutch: sdp.
Transmission: 4F1R, manual a/s.
Final Drive: rear wheels.
Brakes: drum front and rear.
Steering: rack and pinion.
Suspension: front independent coil springs, rear leaf springs.
Tyres: 145 10 radial.
Dimensions, length: 3327mm (10ft 11in); width: 1422mm (4ft 8in); height: 1397mm (4ft 7in); wheelbase: 2146mm (7ft 0.5in); weight-unladen: 504 kg (1114 lb).
Capacities, engine sump: 3.13 litres (5.5 Imp. pints); fuel tank: 27.3 litres (6 Imp. gal); cooling system: 3.4 litres (6 Imp. pints).
Notes: Four wheel model incorporating units used on Reliant three wheeler range. Fibreglass body. Available as saloon and estate.

RELIANT (GB)

ROBIN

850cc

Chassis: separate frame.
Engine: front-mounted, four-cylinder, in-line, ohv, water-cooled, bore 62.5mm, stroke 69.09mm, output 40 bhp at 5500 rev/min, torque 6.3 kgf.m (46 lbf.ft) at 3500 rev/min, compression ratio: 9.5:1.
Carburettor: SU, single.
Clutch: sdp.
Transmission: 4F1R, manual a/s.
Final Drive: rear wheels.
Brakes: drum front and rear.
Steering: rack and pinion.
Suspension: front independent coil springs, rear leaf springs.
Tyres: 145 10 radial.
Dimensions, length: 3327mm (10ft 10.9in); width: 1422mm (4ft 8in); height: 1372mm (4ft 6in); wheelbase: 2159mm (7ft 1in); weight-unladen: 436 kg (962 lb).
Capacities, engine sump: 3.13 litres (5.5 Imp. pints); fuel tank: 27.3 litres (6 Imp. gal); cooling system: 3.4 litres (6 Imp. pints).
   Notes: Introduced in 1973. Original 750cc engine has been uprated to 850cc and is also used in the Kitten.

RELIANT (GB)

SCIMITAR GTE

2994cc

Chassis: separate frame.
Engine: front-mounted, six-cylinder, v-configuration, ohv, water-cooled, bore 93.67mm, stroke 72.4mm, output 135 bhp at 5000 rev/min, torque 23.8 kgf.m (172 lbf.ft) at 3000 rev/min, compression ratio: 8.9:1.
Carburettor: Weber, twin.
Clutch: diaphragm, sdp.
Transmission: 4F1R, manual a/s, 3F1R automatic.
Final Drive: rear wheels.
Brakes: front disc, rear drum, servo-assisted.
Steering: rack and pinion, power-assistance optional.
Suspension: coil springs front and rear.
Tyres: 185HR 14.
Dimensions, length: 4432mm (14ft 2.5in); width: 1708mm (5ft 7.25in); height: 1321m (4ft 4in); wheelbase: 2638mm (8ft 8in); weight-unladen: 1253 kg (2762 lb).
Capacities, engine sump: 5.4 litres (9.5 Imp. pints); fuel tank: 91 litres (20 Imp. gal); cooling system: 11.4 litres (20 Imp. pints).
   Notes: Introduced 1968. Modified September 1975 with wider body and longer wheelbase. Max. speed 193 km/h (120 mph) approx. Manual transmission incorporates overdrive. Glass fibre body. Ford (GB) engine.

RENAULT (F)

Chassis: unitary construction.
Engine: front-mounted, four-cylinder, in-line, ohv, water-cooled, bore 58mm, stroke 80mm, output 34 bhp at 5000 rev/min, torque 5.9 kgf.m. (42.7 lbf.ft) at 2500 rev/min, compression ratio: 8.0:1.
Carburettor: Solex, single.
Clutch: diaphragm, sdp.
Transmission: 4F1R, manual, a/s.
Final Drive: front wheels.
Brakes: drums front and rear.
Steering: rack and pinion.
Suspension: independent torsion bars front and rear.
Tyres: 135SR13.
Dimensions, length: 3683mm (12ft 1in); width: 1486mm (4ft 10.5in); height: 1549mm (5ft 1in); wheelbase: R.H. 2438mm (8ft 0in), L.H. 2400mm (7ft 10.5in); weight-unladen: 695 kg (1532 lb).
Capacities, engine sump: 2.5 litres (4.5 Imp. pints); fuel tank: 34 litres (7.5 Imp. gal); cooling system: 5.5 litres (9.75 Imp. pints).
   Notes: Introduced 1961. The 5-door 4 and 4TL models are continued with detail modifications include double-circuit braking with pressure drop indicator, a new air entry system, anti-theft steering lock and improved windscreen wipers.

RENAULT (F)

Chassis: unitary construction.
Engine: front-mounted, four-cylinder, in-line, water-cooled, bore 70mm, stroke 72mm, output 47 bhp at 5500 rev/min, torque 7.9 kgf.m. (57 lbf.ft) at 3000 rev/min, compression ratio 9.5:1
Carburettor: Solex, single.
Clutch: diaphragm, sdp.
Transmission: 4F1R, manual, a/s.
Final Drive: front wheels.
Brakes: disc front, drum rear.
Steering: rack and pinion.
Suspension: independent torsion bars front and rear.
Tyres: 145 x 13.
Dimensions, length: 3864mm (12ft 8in); width: 1505mm (4ft 11.25in); height: 1475mm (4ft 10in); wheelbase: R.H. 2438mm (8ft 0in), L.H. 2400mm (7ft 10.5in); weight-unladen: 820 kg (1808 lb).
Capacities, engine sump: 3 litres (5.25 Imp. pints); fuel tank: 40 litres (8.75 Imp. gal); cooling system: 6.3 litres (11 Imp. pints).
    Notes: Introduced 1968. Range comprises 6L (845cc, 34 bhp engine) and 6TL (shown). Latest versions have detail modifications including double circuit braking with pressure drop indicator and a number of interior improvements.

RENAULT (F)

14TL   **1218cc**

Chassis: unitary construction.
Engine: front-mounted, four-cylinder, in-line, ohv, water-cooled, bore 75mm, stroke 69mm, output 57 bhp at 6000 rev/min, torque 9.4 kgf.m. (68 lbf.ft) at 3000 rev/min, compression ratio 9.3:1.
Carburettor: Solex, single.
Clutch: diaphragm, sdp.
Transmission: 4F1R, manual, a/s.
Final Drive: front wheels.
Brakes: disc front, drum rear, servo-assisted.
Steering: rack and pinion.
Suspension: independent coil springs front, independent torsion bars rear.
Tyres: 145SR 13.
Dimensions, length: 4025mm (13ft 2in); width: 1624mm (5ft 3in); height: 1405mm (4ft 6in); wheelbase: R.H. 2498mm (8ft 2in); L.H. 2530mm (8ft 3in); weight: 865 kg (1907 lb).
Capacities, engine sump: 4 litres (7 Imp. pints); fuel tank: 48 litres (10.5 Imp. gal); cooling system: 6 litres (10.5 imp. pints).
   Notes: Introduced 1976 (1977 UK). Five-door hatchback powered by a Renault/Peugeot transverse-mounted engine, and produced in France and Belgium. Latest version has double-circuit braking with pressure drop indicator, larger fuel tank and detail interior modifications.

RENAULT (F)

5GTL   **1289cc**

Chassis: unitary construction.
Engine: front-mounted, four-cylinder, in-line, ohv, water-cooled, bore 73mm, stroke 77mm, output 44 bhp at 5000 rev/min, torque 8.6 kgf.m. (62.2 lbf.ft) at 2000 rev/min, compression ratio 9.5:1.
Carburettor: Solex, single.
Clutch: diaphragm, sdp.
Transmission: 4F1R manual, a/s.
Final Drive: front wheels.
Brakes: disc front, drum rear, servo-assisted.
Steering: rack and pinion.
Suspension: independent torsion bars front and rear.
Tyres: 145 13.
Dimensions, length: 3500mm (11ft 6in); width: 1520 mm (5ft 0in); height: 1397mm (4ft 7in); Wheelbase: R.H. 7ft 10.675in , L.H. 7ft 11.75in ; weight: 785 kg (1730 lb).
Capacities, engine sump: 3 litres (5.25 Imp. pints); fuel tank: 37.5 litres (8.25 Imp. gal.); cooling system: 6.3 litres (11 Imp. pints).
   Notes: Introduced 1972 (UK). Range comprises 5L (845cc, 36 bhp engine) 5TL (956cc, 44 bhp engine) 5GTL (shown) and 5TS (1289cc, 64 bhp engine). Latest versions have a number of modifications including double-circuit braking (servo-assisted on 5GTL) improved windscreen wipers and pivot-opening rear windows (5TL and 5GTL).

RENAULT (F)

12TS **1289cc**

Chassis: unitary construction.
Engine: front-mounted, four-cylinder, in-line, ohv, water-cooled, bore 73mm, stroke 77mm, output 60 bhp at 5500 rev/min, torque 9.3 kgf.m. (67.2 lbf.ft) at 3500 rev/min, compression ratio 9.5:1.
Carburettor: Weber, single.
Clutch: diaphragm, sdp.
Transmission: 4F1R, manual, a/s.
Final Drive: front wheels.
Brakes: disc front, drum rear.
Steering: rack and pinion.
Suspension: independent coil springs front, coil springs rear.
Tyres: 4.50B x 13.
Dimensions, length: 4345mm (14ft 3in); width: 1610mm (5ft 3.5in); height: 1430mm (4ft 8.5in); wheelbase: 2440mm (8ft 0in); weight: 935 kg (2061 lb).
Capacities, engine sump: 3 litres (5.25 Imp. pints); fuel tank: 46.5 litres (10.25 Imp. gal); cooling system: 5 litres (8.75 Imp. pints).
  Notes: Introduced 1970 (UK) and restyled in 1975. Range comprises 12L (50 bhp engine) 12TL (saloon and estate — 54 bhp engine) — 12TS (shown) and 12 Auto (60 bhp engine). Latest versions have a number of modifications including double circuit braking with pressure drop indicator and various interior improvements.

RENAULT (F)

15GTL   **1289cc**

Chassis: unitary construction.
Engine: front-mounted, four-cylinder, in-line, ohv, water-cooled,
bore 73mm, stroke 77mm, output 60 bhp at 5500 rev/min,
torque 9.3 kgf.m. (67.2 lbf.ft) at 3500 rev/min, compression
ratio 9.5:1.
Carburettor: Weber, single.
Clutch: diaphragm, sdp.
Transmission: 4F1R, manual, a/s; 3F1R automatic optional.
Final Drive: front wheels.
Brakes: disc front, drum rear, servo-assisted.
Steering: rack and pinion.
Suspension: independent coil springs front, coil springs rear.
Tyres: 155SR 13.
Dimensions, length: 4262mm (13ft 11.5in); width: 1630mm (5ft
4.25in); height: 1310mm (4ft 3.5in); wheelbase: 2440mm
(8ft 0in); weight-unladen: 965 kg (2128 lb).
Capacities, engine sump: 3 litres (5.25 Imp. pints); fuel tank:
55 litres (12 Imp. gal); cooling system: 5 litres (8.75 Imp. pints).
   Notes: Introduced 1971, (restyled 1976). Two-door sports
coupé the latest version of which has a number of detail modifications including new style wheels and seats. Maximum speed
150 km/h (93 mph).

RENAULT (F)

16TX   **1647cc**

Chassis: unitary construction.
Engine: front-mounted, four-cylinder, in-line, ohv, water-cooled, bore 79mm, stroke 84mm, output 93 bhp at 6000 rev/min, torque 13.11 kgf.m (94.8 lbf.ft) at 4000 rev/min, compression ratio 9.25:1.
Carburettor: weber, single.
Clutch: diaphragm, sdp.
Transmission: 4F1R, manual, a/s; 3F1R automatic optional.
Final Drive: front wheels.
Brakes: disc front, drum rear, servo-assisted.
Steering: rack and pinion.
Suspension: independent torsion bars front and rear.
Tyres: 155SR14.
Dimensions, length: 4235mm (13ft 10.75in); width: 1626mm (5ft 4in); height: 1448mm (4ft 9in); wheelbase: R.H. 2648mm (8ft 8.25in); L.H. 2718mm (8ft 11in); weight: 1060 kg (2337 lb).
Capacities, engine sump: 4 litres (7 Imp. pints); fuel tank: 50 litres (11 Imp. gal); cooling system: 6.8 litres (12 Imp. pints).
    Notes: Top model in the '16' range, which was introduced in 1965. Also available on the UK market is the 16TL powered by a 1565cc, 65 bhp engine, with either manual or automatic transmission.

RENAULT (F)

20TS   **1995cc**

Chassis: unitary construction.
Engine: front-mounted, four-cylinder, in-line, ohc, water-cooled, bore 88mm, stroke 82mm, output 110 bhp at 5500 rev/min, torque 17 kgf.m. (127 lbf.ft) at 3000 rev/min, compression ratio 9.2:1.
Carburettor: Weber, single.
Clutch: diaphragm, sdp.
Transmission: 4F1R, manual, a/s; 3F1R automatic optional.
Final Drive: front wheels.
Brakes: disc front, drum rear, servo-assisted.
Steering: rack and pinion, power assisted.
Suspension: independent coil springs front and rear.
Tyres: 165SR14.
Dimensions, length: 4520mm (14ft 10in); width: 1730mm (5ft 8in); height: 1440mm (4ft 8in); wheelbase: 2670mm (8ft 9in); weight: 1260 kg (2778 lb).
Capacities, engine sump: 5 litres (8.75 Imp. pints); fuel tank: 67 litres (14.75 Imp. gal); cooling systems: 9.75 litres (17.25 Imp. pints).
   Notes: Introduced 1977. Has the same 5-door hatchback body shell and technical layout as the 30TS and 20TL. Specification includes — power steering, electric front windows, tinted glass and electro-magnetic door locks. Maximum speed 168 km/h (105 mph).

RENAULT (F)

30 TS   **2664cc**

Chassis: unitary construction.
Engine: front-mounted, six-cylinder, V-configuration, water-cooled, bore 88mm, stroke 73mm, output 131 bhp at 5500 rev/min, torque 20.5 kgf.m (148.3 lbf.ft) at 2500 rev/min, compression ratio 8.65:1.
Carburettor: Weber, single.
Clutch: diaphragm, sdp.
Transmission: 4F1R, manual, a/s; 3F1R automatic optional.
Final Drive: front wheels.
Brakes: discs front and rear, servo-assisted.
Steering: rack and pinion, power-assisted.
Suspension: independent, coil springs front and rear.
Tyres: 175 SR 14.
Dimensions, length: 4520mm (14ft 10in); width: 1730mm (5ft 8in); height: 1440mm (4ft 8in); wheelbase: 2670mm (8ft 9in); weight: 1320 kg (2910 lb).
Capacities, engine sump: 5.5 litres (9.75 Imp. pints); fuel tank: 67 litres (14.75 Imp. gal); cooling system: 9.75 litres (17.25 Imp. pints).
   Notes: Introduced 1975. Five-door saloon, powered by a Renault-Peugeot-Volvo V-6 engine and incorporating, on the latest version, larger rubber overriders — front and rear, rear seat head restraints, electronic ignition (30 TS Automatic).

RENAULT (F)

20TL   **1647cc**

Chassis: unitary construction.
Engine: front-mounted, four-cylinder, in-line, ohv, water-cooled, bore 79mm, stroke 84mm, output 90 bhp at 5750 rev/min, torque 13.4 kgf.m (96.9 lbf.ft) at 3500 rev/min, compression ratio: 9.3:1.
Carburettor: Weber, single.
Clutch: sdp.
Transmission: 4F1R, manual, a/s; 3F1R automatic optional.
Final Drive: front wheels.
Brakes: disc front, drum rear, servo-assisted.
Steering: rack and pinion.
Suspension: independent coil springs front, independent torsion bar rear.
Tyres: 165 SR x 13.
Dimensions, length: 4520mm (14ft 10in); width: 1730mm (5ft 8in); height: 1440mm (4ft 8in); wheelbase: 2670mm (8ft 9in); weight-unladen: 1165 kg (2590 lb).
Capacities, engine sump: 4 litres (7 Imp. pints); fuel tank: 59 litres (13 Imp. gal); cooling system: 7.4 litres (13 Imp. pints).
   Notes: Introduced 1975 (1976 UK). Five-door, 5-seater saloon, the latest version of which incorporates a number of modifications including improved dashboard, new styled wheels, engine improvements and revised tailgate counterbalancing mechanism.

ROLLS-ROYCE (GB)

CAMARGUE   6750cc

Chassis: unitary construction.
Engine: eight-cylinder, V-configuration, ohv, water-cooled, bore 104mm, stroke 99mm, output and torque not disclosed, compression ratio 8:1.
Carburettor: Solex, single.
Clutch: not disclosed.
Transmission: 3F1R automatic.
Final Drive: rear wheels.
Brakes: disc front and rear, power-assisted.
Steering: rack and pinion, power-assisted.
Suspension: independent coil spring front and rear.
Tyres: HR 70, HR 15 or 235/70 HR 15.
Dimensions, length: 5170mm (16ft 11.5in); width: 1920mm (6ft 3.5in); height: 1470mm (4ft 10in); wheelbase: 3050mm (10ft 0in); weight-unladen: 2330 kg (5135 lb).
Capacities, engine sump: 8 litres (14.5 Imp. pints); fuel tank: 107 litres (23.5 Imp. gal); cooling system: 16 litres (28.5 Imp. pints).
   Notes: Two-door five-seater saloon introduced 1975. Designed by Pininfarina. Latest version has a number of modifications including new steering and fully automatic, two-level air conditioning system.

ROLLS-ROYCE (GB)

SILVER SHADOW II   6750cc

Chassis: unitary construction.
Engine: eight-cylinder, V-configuration, ohv, water-cooled, bore 104mm, stroke 99mm, output and torque not disclosed, compression ratio 8:1.
Carburettor: SU, twin.
Clutch: N.A.
Transmission: 3F1R automatic.
Final Drive: rear wheels.
Brakes: disc front and rear, power-assisted.
Steering: rack and pinion, power-assisted.
Suspension: independent coil spring front and rear.
Tyres: HR 70, HR 15 or 235/70 HR 15.
Dimensions, length: 5169mm (16ft 11.5in); width: 1918mm (6ft 3.5in); height: 1473mm (4ft 10in); wheelbase: 3048mm (10ft 0 in); weight: 2329 kg (5135 lb).
Capacities, engine sump: 8 litres (14.5 Imp. pints); fuel tank: 107 litres (23.5 Imp. gal); cooling system: 16 litres (28.5 Imp. pints).
   Notes: The 'II' version is distinguishable from the original Silver Shadow by more than 2000 improvements, the latest of which include new steering, revised suspension, restyled fascia and a new air conditioning system. Similar specification to the Bentley T2.

ROLLS-ROYCE (GB)

SILVER WRAITH II   6750cc

Chassis: unitary construction.
Engine: front-mounted, eight-cylinder, V-configuration, ohv, water-cooled, bore 104mm, stroke 99mm, output not disclosed, torque not disclosed, compression ratio 8.0:1.
Carburettor: SU, twin.
Clutch: N.A.
Transmission: 3F1R, automatic.
Final Drive: rear wheels.
Brakes: disc front and rear, servo-assisted.
Steering: rack and pinion, power assisted.
Suspension: independent coil springs front and rear.
Tyres: HR 70, HR 15 or 235/70 HR 15.
Dimensions, length: 5300mm (17ft 4.5in); width: 1800mm (5ft 11in); height: 1520mm (4ft 11.75in); wheelbase: 3124mm (10ft 4in); weight: 2278 kg (5020 lb).
Capacities, engine sump: 8.0 litres (14.5 Imp. pints); fuel tank: 107 litres (23.5 Imp. gals); cooling system: 16.0 litres (28.5 Imp. pints).
  Notes: The Silver Wraith II, announced early in 1977. Marks the reappearance of a famous Rolls-Royce model name first introduced some forty years ago. Longest of the four-door saloons, it incorporates the usual Rolls-Royce features and is also available with an electrically operated glass division.

SAAB (S)

99 GLE   1985cc

Chassis: unitary construction.
Engine: front-mounted, four-cylinder, in-line, ohc, water-cooled, bore 90mm, stroke 78mm, output 118 bhp at 5500 rev/min, torque 17 kgf.m (123 lbf.ft) at 3700 rev/min, compression ratio 9.2:1.
Carburettor: N.A. (fuel inj.).
Clutch: diaphragm, sdp.
Transmission: 3FIR, automatic.
Final drive: front wheels.
Brakes: disc front and rear, servo-assisted.
Steering: rack and pinion (power-assisted on L.H.D.).
Suspension: independent coil springs, front and rear.
Tyres: 165 SRx15
Dimensions, length: 4420mm (14ft 6in); width: 1690mm (5ft 6.5in); height: 1440mm (4ft 8.75in); wheelbase: 2473mm (8ft 1.5in); weight-unladen 1220kg (2670lb).
Capacities, Engine Sump: 3.5 litres (6.25 Imp. pints); fuel tank: 55 litres (12 Imp gal); Cooling System: 8 litres (14 Imp. pints).
   Notes: Introduced 1976. The 99 GLE is the top specification in the 99 range, the other models being 99L, 99GL and 99 EMS. The EMS incorporates fuel injection equipment and 118 bhp engine. The L and GL feature Stromberg carburretors and 100/108 bhp engine. Latest 99GLE incorporates a number of new features including five-door styling, improved forward visibility and other interior modifications.
The EMS is similar, but has three doors.

SKODA (CS)

ESTELLE 120L   **1174cc**

Chassis: unitary construction.
Engine: rear-mounted, four-cylinder, in-line ohv, water-cooled, bore 72mm, stroke 72mm, output 52 bhp at 5000 rev/min, torque 8.7 kgf.m (62.9 lbf.ft) at 3250 rev/min, compression ratio 8.5:1.
Carburettor: EDSR, single.
Clutch: sdp.
Transmission: 4F1R, manual, a/s.
Final Drive: rear wheels.
Brakes: disc front, drum rear.
Steering: worm and nut.
Suspension: independent coil spring front, coil spring rear.
Tyres: 155 14.
Dimensions, length: 4160mm (13ft 7.75in); width: 1595mm (5ft 2.75in); height: 1400mm (4ft 7in); wheelbase: 2400mm (7ft 10.5in); weight: 875 kg (1929 lb).
Capacities, engine sump: 4 litres (7 Imp. pints); fuel tank: 38 litres (8.5 Imp. gal); cooling system: 12 litres (22 Imp. pints).
   Notes: Introduced 1977. The first major car launch from Czechoslovakia for ten years. Four model range, which replaces the 'S' type, comprises the 105S and 105L (1046cc 46 bhp engine), the 120L (shown) and the 120LS (1174cc 58 bhp engine). Twin headlamps distinguish, externally, the 120LS from the other models.

SKODA (CS)

S110R Coupe

1107cc

Chassis: unitary construction.
Engine: rear-mounted, four-cylinder, in-line, ohv, water-cooled, bore 72mm, stroke 68mm, output 52 bhp at 4650 rev/min, torque 8.8 kgf.m (64 lbf.ft) at 3500 rev/min, compression ratio 9.5:1.
Carburettor: Jikov, single.
Clutch: sdp.
Transmission: 4F1R manual, a/s.
Final Drive: rear wheels.
Brakes: disc front, drum rear.
Steering: worm and peg.
Suspension. independent coil springs front, coil springs rear.
Tyres: 155 SR 14.
Dimensions, length: 4155mm (13ft 7.5in); width: 1620mm (5ft 3.75in); height: 1340mm (4ft 4.75in); wheelbase: 2400mm (7ft 10.5in); weight-unladen: 880 kg (1940 lb).
Capacities, engine sump: 4.75 litres (8.25 Imp. pints); fuel tank: 32 litres (7 Imp. gal); cooling system: 6.9 litres (12 Imp. pints).
Notes: Introduced 1970. Maximum speed 145 kph (90 mph). Continued as the only 'S' model, following the introduction of the Estelle. Coupé body styling and special wheel trims give easy identification.

SUBARU (J)

STATION WAGON   1600cc

Chassis: unitary construction.
Engine: front-mounted, four-cylinder, horizontally opposed, ohv, water-cooled.
Carburretor: Hitachi, twin.
Clutch: diaphragm, sdp.
Transmission: 4FIR, manual, a/s.
Final Drive: all wheels.
Steering: rack and pinion.
Tyres: 155 SR 13.
Dimensions, length: 4026mm (13ft 2.5in); width: 1550mm (5ft 1in); height: 1441mm (4ft 8.75in); wheelbase: 2439mm (8ft 0.5in); weight-unladen: 968 kg (2150 lb).
Capacities, engine sump: 3.4 litres (6 Imp. pints); fuel tank; 45.5 litres (10 Imp. gal).

   Notes: Four-wheel drive estate model — one of new range of Japanese cars introduced onto the U.K. market in 1977. Also available are 1600 Coupé and 1600 Hardtop models.

TOYOTA (J)

1000   **993cc**

Chassis: unitary construction.
Engine: front-mounted, four-cylinder, in-line, ohv, water-cooled, bore 72mm, stroke 61mm, output 47 bhp at 5800 rev/min, torque 6.5 kgf.m. (48 lbf.ft) at 3800 rev/min, compression ratio 9.0:1.
Carburettor: Aisan, single.
Clutch: diaphragm, sdp.
Transmission: 4FIR, manual, a/s.
Final Drive: rear wheels.
Brakes: disc front, drum rear, servo-assisted.
Steering: recirculating ball.
Suspension: independent coil springs front, leaf springs rear.
Tyres: 155 SR x 12.
Dimensions, length: 3702mm (12ft 1.75in); width: 1450mm (4ft 9.5in); height: 1409mm (4ft 7.5in); wheelbase: 2160mm (7ft 1in); weight-unladen: 734 kg (1631 lb).
Capacities, engine sump: 5 litres (2.8 Imp. pints); fuel tank: 40 litres (9 Imp. gal); cooling system: 4.7 litres (8.25 Imp. pints).
  Notes: Introduced in the U.K. 1974 (saloon); 1976 (estate – shown). Maximum speed of the estate 135 km/h (84mph). Tinted windscreen and front door windows standard on the estate (all round on the saloon).

COROLLA 30 **1166cc**

Chassis: unitary construction.
Engine: front-mounted, four-cylinder, in-line, ohv, water-cooled, bore 75mm, stroke 66mm, output 56 bhp at 6000 rev/min, torque 8.5 kgf.m (61 lbf.ft) at 3800 rev/min, compression ratio 9.0:1.
Carburettor: Aisan, single.
Clutch: diaphragm, sdp.
Transmission: 4FIR, manual, a/s; 2FIR automatic optional.
Final Drive: rear wheels.
Brakes: disc front, drum rear, servo-assisted.
Steering: recirculating ball.
Suspension: independent coil springs front, leaf springs rear.
Tyres: 155 SR x 13.
Dimensions, length: 3994mm (13 ft 1.25 in); width: 1568mm (5ft 1.75in); height: 1370mm (4ft 6in); wheelbase: 2368mm (7ft 9.25in); weight-unladen: 870 kg (1935 lb).
Capacities, engine sump: 3.7 litres (6.5 Imp pints); fuel tank: 50 litres (11 Imp. gal); cooling system: 4.5 litres (8 Imp. pints).
  Notes: Introduced 1975 (U.K.). Range comprises 2-door and 4-door saloons, estate and 1200 and 1600 (1588cc, 73 bhp engine), liftbacks. Latest versions have minor styling changes and other detail modifications.

CARINA   1588cc

Chassis: unitary construction.
Engine: front-mounted, four-cylinder, in-line, ohv, water-cooled, bore 85mm, stroke 70mm, output 75 bhp at 5200 rev/min, torque 11.7 kgf.m (85.3 lbf.ft) at 3800 rev/min, compression ratio 9.0:1.
Carburettor: Aisan, single.
Clutch: sdp.
Transmission: 4 FIR, manual, a/s; 3 FIR automatic optional.
Final Drive: rear wheels.
Brakes: disc front, drum rear, servo-assisted.
Steering: recirculating ball.
Suspension: independent coil springs front, coil springs rear.
Tyres: 165 x 13.
Dimensions, length: 4200mm (13ft 9.25in); width: 1590mm (5ft 2.75in); height: 1385mm (4ft 6.5in); wheelbase: 2495mm (8ft 2.25in); weight 995 kg (2192 lb).
Capacities, engine sump: 3.7 litres (6.5 Imp. pints); fuel tank: 58 litres (12.75 Imp. gal); cooling system: 8.5 litres (15 Imp. pints).
  Notes: Maximum speed 160 km/h (100 mph). Specification includes tinted glass all-round, reclining front seats with head restraints, radio and clock.

TOYOTA (J)

CELICA
1588cc

Chassis: unitary construction.
Engine: front-mounted, four-cylinder, in-line, ohc, water-cooled, bore 85mm, stroke 70mm, output 104 bhp at 6200 rev/min, torque 13.1 kgf.m (95 lbf.ft) at 5200 rev/min, compression ratio 9.8:1.
Carburettor: Mikuni Solex, two.
Clutch: sdp.
Transmission: 5FIR, manual, a/s.
Final Drive: rear wheels.
Brakes: disc front, drum rear, servo-assisted.
Steering: recirculating ball.
Suspension: independent coil springs front, coil springs rear.
Tyres: 185/70 HR 13.
Dimensions: length: 4260mm (13ft 11.75in); width: 1615mm (5ft 3.75in); height: 1310mm (4ft 3.5in); wheelbase: 2495mm (8ft 2.25in); weight: 1005kg (2235lb).
Capacities, engine sump: 3.7 litres (6.5 Imp. pints); fuel tank: 58 litres (12.75 Imp. gall); cooling system: 8.5 litres (15 Imp. pints).
   Note: The Celica line-up comprises the 1600 GT Coupé (shown), 1600 ST Coupé (1588cc, ohv, 86 bhp engine), 2000 ST Coupé and Liftback (1968cc, 86 bhp engine) and 2000 GT Liftback (1968cc, 118 bhp engine).

CRESSIDA SALOON

1968cc

Chassis: unitary construction.
Engine: front-mounted, four-cylinder, in-line, ohc, water-cooled, bore 88.5mm, stroke 80mm, output 89 bhp at 5000 rev/min, torque 14.8 kgf.m (107 lbf.ft) at 3600 rev/min, compression ratio 8.5:1.
Carburettor: Nikki, single.
Clutch: diaphragm, sdp.
Transmission: 4F1R, manual, a/s; 3F1R automatic optional.
Final Drive: rear wheels.
Brakes: disc front, drum rear, servo-assisted.
Steering: recirculating ball.
Suspension: independent coil springs front, coil springs rear.
Tyres: 175 SR 14.
Dimensions, length: 4528mm (14ft 10.25in); width: 1676mm (5ft 6in); height: 1448mm (4ft 9in); wheelbase: 2642mm (8ft 8in); weight-unladen: 1090 kg (2403 lb).
Capacities, fuel tank: 65 litres (14.25 Imp. gal).
   Notes: Introduced 1977 (U.K.). Replaces the 2000 model which was introduced in Britain as an interim model in 1975. Maximum speed 160 km/h (100 mph). Estate version has similar specification but fitted with uprated leaf spring rear suspension.

TOYOTA (J)

CROWN SUPER

2563cc

Chassis: unitary construction.
Engine: front-mounted, six-cylinder, in-line, ohc, water-cooled, bore 80mm, stroke 85mm, output 118 bhp at 5000 rev/min, torque 19.8 kgf.m (143 lbf.ft) at 3000 rev/min, compression ratio 9.2:1.
Carburettor: Aisan, single.
Clutch: N.A.
Transmission: 3F1R, automatic.
Final Drive: rear wheels.
Brakes: disc front, drum rear, servo-assisted.
Steering: recirculating ball, power-assisted.
Suspension: independent coil springs front, coil springs rear.
Tyres: 185 SR 14.
Dimensions, length: 4686mm (15ft 4.5in); width: 1695mm (5ft 6.75in); height: 1535mm (4ft 8.5in); wheelbase: 2690mm (8ft 10in); weight: 1415 kg (3120 lb).
Capacities, engine sump: 5.2 litres (9.25 Imp. pints); fuel tank: 71 litres (15.75 Imp. gal); cooling system: 11 litres (19.5 Imp. pints).

  Notes: Also available as estate car. Latest versions feature styling changes — new front grille, lowered bonnet — new side mouldings — engine modifications, improved automatic transmission and power-assisted steering, and modified instrumentation.

TVR (GB)

3000M

2994cc

Chassis: tubular frame.
Engine: front-mounted, six-cylinder, v-configuration, ohv, water-cooled, bore 94mm, stroke 72.4mm, output 142 bhp at 5000 rev/min, torque 23.7 kgf.m (172 lbf.ft) at 3000 rev/min, compression ratio: 8.9:1.
Carburettor: Weber, single.
Clutch: diaphragm, sdp.
Transmission: 4F1R, manual a/s.
Final Drive: rear wheels.
Brakes: disc front, drum rear, servo-assisted.
Steering: rack and pinion.
Suspension: independent coil springs front and rear.
Tyres: 185 HR 14.
Dimensions, length: 3937mm (12ft 11in); width: 1626mm (5ft 4in); height: 1143mm (3ft 11In); wheelbase: 2286mm (7ft 6in); weight unladen: 990 kg (2184 lb).
Capacities, engine sump: 5 litres (8.75 Imp. pints); fuel tank: 54 litres (12 Imp. gal); cooling system: 11 litres (19 Imp. pints).
   Notes: Introduced 1972; re-styled body autumn 1976. Also available are the 2500M, Turbo (230 bhp engine), Taimar (142 bhp engine) and Taimar Turbo (230 bhp engine) models. The two Taimar models have an upward opening tailgate.

VAUXHALL (GB)

CHEVETTE ESTATE

1256cc

Chassis: unitary construction.
Engine: front-mounted, four-cylinder, in-line, ohv, water-cooled, bore 80.97mm, stroke 60.96mm, output 58 bhp at 5600 rev/min, torque 9.3 kgf.m (66.5 lbf.ft) at 2600 rev/min, compression ratio: 9.2:1.
Carburettor: Stromberg, single.
Clutch: diaphragm, sdp.
Transmission: 4F1R, manual a/s.
Final Drive: rear wheels.
Brakes: disc front, drum rear, servo-assisted.
Steering: rack and pinion.
Suspension: independent coil springs front, coil springs rear.
Tyres: 155SR 13.
Dimensions, length: 4178mm (13ft 8.5in); width: 1570mm (5ft 1.75in); height: 1308mm (4ft 3in); wheelbase: 2396mm (7ft 10.25in); weight-unladen: 4302kg (1951 lb).
Capacities, engine sump: 3.1 litres (5.5 Imp. pints); fuel tank: 45 litres (9.5 Imp. gal); cooling system: 5.8 litres (10 Imp. pints).
   Notes: Introduced 1975 (Hatchback) 1976 (Saloon/Estate). Range comprises 3-door E, L, GL, GLS Hatchbacks, 2-door E, L and 4-door E, L and GLS Saloons, and 3-door Estate (shown).

VAUXHALL (GB)

VIVA 1300 GLS

1256cc

Chassis: unitary construction.
Engine: front-mounted, four-cylinder, in-line, ohv, water-cooled, bore 80.97mm, stroke 60.96mm, output 58 bhp at 5600 rev/min, torque 9.3 kgf.m (66.5 lbf.ft) at 2600 rev/min, compression ratio: 9.2:1.
Carburettor: Stromberg, single.
Clutch: diaphragm, sdp.
Transmission: 4F1R, manual a/s.
Final Drive: rear wheels.
Brakes: disc front, drum rear, servo-assisted.
Steering: rack and pinion.
Suspension: independent coil springs front, coil springs rear.
Tyres: 155SR 13.
Dimensions, length: 4137mm (13ft 7in); width: 1643mm (5ft 4.75in); height: 1351mm (4ft 5.25in); wheelbase: 2461mm (8ft 1in); weight-unladen: 910 kg (2006 lb).
Capacities, engine sump: 3.1 litres (5.5 Imp. pints); fuel tank: 36 litres (8 Imp. gal); cooling system: 5.8 litres (10.25 Imp. pints).
   Notes: Current series (HC) introduced 1970. Max. speed 137 km/h (85 mph). Range comprises 2- and 4-door E, 1300L, 1800L (1759cc engine) and GLS Saloons and 1300 GLS Estate. Automatic transmission available with '1800' engine.

VAUXHALL (GB)

CAVALIER GLS COUPE   1897cc

Chassis: unitary construction.
Engine: front-mounted, four-cylinder, in-line, ohc, water-cooled, bore 93mm, stroke 69.8mm, output 90 bhp at 4800 rev/min, torque 14.5 kgf.m (105 lbf.ft) at 3800 rev/min, compression ratio: 8.8:1.
Carburettor: Solex, single.
Clutch: diaphragm, sdp.
Transmission: 4F1R, manual a/s, optional 3F1R automatic.
Final Drive: rear wheels.
Brakes: disc front, drum rear, servo-assisted.
Steering: rack and pinion.
Suspension: independent coil springs front, coil springs rear.
Tyres: 185SR 13.
Dimensions, length: 4496mm (14ft 9in); width: 1650mm (5ft 4.75in); height: 1330mm (4ft 4.5in); wheelbase: 2518mm (8ft 3in); weight-unladen: 1010 kg (2227 lb).
Capacities, engine sump: 3.8 litres (6.7 Imp. pints); fuel tank: 50 litres (11 Imp. gall); cooling system: 7 litres (12 Imp. pints).
  Notes: Introduced in October 1975. Top of the range sports coupé with luxury trim. Front end distinguished from Cavalier saloons by air dam. Two- and four-door L 1300, L 1600S and GL 1600S and four-door GL 1900S saloon models available.

VAUXHALL (GB)

MAGNUM

2279cc

Chassis: unitary construction.
Engine: front-mounted, four-cylinder, in-line, ohc, water-cooled, bore 97.54mm, stroke 76.2mm, output 108 bhp at 5000 rev/min, torque 19 kgf.m (138 lbf.ft) at 3000 rev/min, compression ratio: 8.5:1.
Carburettor: Stromberg, single.
Clutch: diaphragm, sdp.
Transmission: 4F1R, manual a/s, optional 3F1R automatic.
Final Drive: rear wheels.
Brakes: disc front, drum rear, servo-assisted.
Steering: rack and pinion.
Suspension: independent coil springs front, coil springs rear.
Tyres: 175SR 13.
Dimensions, length: 4153mm (13ft 7.5in); width: 1643mm (5ft 4.75in); height: 1366mm (4ft 4.5in); wheelbase: 2461mm (8ft 1in); weight-unladen; 1077 kg (2374 lb).
Capacities, engine sump: 4.8 litres (8.5 Imp. pints); fuel tank: 54 litres (12 Imp. gal); cooling system: 8.2 litres (14.5 Imp. pints).
   Notes: Introduced 1973. Available in two-door and four-door saloons and estate car versions. 1759cc (88 bhp) engine also available. Similar appearance to Viva GLS models.

VAUXHALL (GB)

VX 4/90 **2279cc**

Chassis: unitary construction.
Engine: front-mounted, four-cylinder, in-line, ohc, water-cooled, bore 97.54mm, stroke 76.2mm, output 116 bhp at 5000 rev/min, torque 20 kgf.m (145 lbf.ft) at 3000 rev/min, compression ratio: 8.5:1.
Carburettor: Stromberg, two.
Clutch: diaphragm, sdp.
Transmission: 5F1R, manual a/s.
Final Drive: rear wheels.
Brakes: disc front, drum rear, servo-assisted.
Steering: rack and pinion.
Suspension: independent coil springs front, coil springs rear.
Tyres: 185 SR 14.
Dimensions, length: 4586mm (16ft 1in); width: 1712mm (5ft 7in); height: 1326mm (4ft 4.25in); wheelbase: 2658mm (8ft 8.5in); weight-unladen: 1245 kg (2745 lb).
Capacities, engine sump: 4.8 litres (8.5 Imp. pints); fuel tank: 65 litres (14.25 Imp. gal); cooling system: 8.2 litres (14.5 Imp. pints).
   Notes: Distinguishable from other models in the VX range by sports road wheels, distinctive grille, black-painted centre pillars and side-window surrounds. Also available in VX range are 1800 (1759cc engine), 2300 (2279cc 108 bhp engine) saloons and estates and 2300 GLS saloon.

171

VOLKSWAGEN (D)

POLO

900cc

Chassis: unitary construction.
Engine: front-mounted, four-cylinder, in-line, ohc, water-cooled, bore 69.5mm stroke 59mm, output 40 bhp at 5900 rev/min, torque 6.3 kgf.m (46 lbf.ft) at 3500 rev/min, compression ratio: 8.5:1.
Carburettor: Solex, single.
Clutch: sdp.
Transmission: 4F1R, manual a/s.
Final Drive: front wheels.
Brakes: disc front, drum rear.
Steering: rack and pinion.
Suspension: independent coil springs front and rear.
Tyres: 135 SR 13.
Dimensions, length: 3512mm (11ft 5in); width: 1599mm (5ft 2in); height: 1296mm (4ft 2.5in); wheelbase: 2330mm (7ft 7in); weight-unladen: 685 kg (1510 lb).
Capacities, engines sump: 3.5 litres (6 Imp. pints); fuel tank: 36 litres (8 Imp. gal); cooling system: 6 litres (11 Imp. pints).
   Notes: Three door saloon designed by Audi NSU and Bertone of Italy. Available with the 900cc engine, are the 'L' and 'N' versions and, with an 1100cc engine, the 'LS' model.

VOLKSWAGEN (D)

GOLF   **1100cc**

Chassis: unitary construction.
Engine: front-mounted, four-cylinder, in-line, ohc, water-cooled, bore 69.5mm, stroke 72mm.
Carburettor: Solex, single.
Clutch: sdp.
Transmission: 4F1R, manual a/s.
Final Drive: front wheels.
Brakes: disc front, drum rear, servo-assisted.
Steering: rack and pinion.
Suspension: coil springs front and rear.
Tyres: 145SR 13.
Dimensions, length: 3705mm (12ft 0.5in); width: 1610mm (5ft 3in); height: 1410mm (4ft 7in); wheelbase: 2400mm (7ft 10in).
   Notes: Introduced 1974. Available as 'N' 3-door, standard trim (shown) and 'L' 5-door, extra trim models.
   Latest versions have revised specifications which include improvements to internal fittings and sound insulation, and the more powerful 'LS' and 'GLS' now have a new 1460cc, 70 bhp engine to replace the previous 1588cc unit.

VOLKSWAGEN (D)

PASSAT

1588cc

Chassis: unitary construction.
Engine: front-mounted, four-cylinder, in-line, ohc, water-cooled, bore 79.5mm, stroke 80mm.
Carburettor: Solex, single.
Clutch: diaphragm, sdp.
Transmission: 4F1R, manual, a/s.
Final Drive: front wheels.
Brakes: disc front, drum rear, servo-assisted.
Steering: rack and pinion.
Suspension: independent coil springs front, coil springs rear.
Tyres: 175 SR 13.
Dimensions, length: 4290mm (13ft 11.25in); width: 1615mm (5ft 3in); height: 1360mm (4ft 5in).
Capacities, engine sump: 3.2 litres (6.25 Imp. pints); fuel tank: 45 litres (10 Imp. gal); cooling system: 6.5 litres (11.25 Imp. pints).
   Notes: Introduced 1973. Latest version has changes to the body and suspension system.

VOLKSWAGEN (D)

SCIROCCO GLS   1588cc

Chassis: unitary construction.
Engine: front-mounted, four-cylinder, in-line, ohc, water-cooled, bore 79.5mm, stroke 80mm, output 85 bhp at 5800 rev/min, torque 12.5 kgf.m (91 lbf.ft) at 3800 rev/min, compression ratio 9.7:1.
Carburettor: Solex, single.
Clutch: diaphragm, sdp.
Transmission: 4F1R, manual a/s (standard); 3F1R automatic (optional).
Final Drive: front wheels.
Brakes: disc front, drum rear, servo-assisted.
Steering: rack and pinion.
Suspension: coil springs front and rear.
Tyres: 175 / 70SR 13.
Dimensions, length: 3885mm (12ft 7.05in); width: 1625mm (5ft 3in); height: 1295mm (4ft 2.05in); wheelbase: 2400mm (7ft 9.05in).

   Notes: Introduced 1974. Styled by Guigiario of Italy . The latest version of this 2 + 2 coupé has certain modifications including body styling changes — particularly noticeable at the front end — and improved running rear. GTI (110 bhp fuel injection) L.H.D. version also available (to special order); as are standard, 'L', 'S' and 'LS' depending on market area.

66 GL

1289cc

Chassis: unitary construction.
Engine: front-mounted, four-cylinder, in-line, ohv, water-cooled, bore 73mm, stroke 77mm, output 57 bhp at 5200 rev/min, torque 10 kgf.m (69 lbf.ft) at 3000 rev/min, compression ratio: 8.5:1.
Carburettor: Solex, single.
Clutch: centrifugal.
Transmission: automatic, variable ratio.
Final Drive: rear wheels.
Brakes: disc front, drum rear, servo-assisted.
Steering: rack and pinion.
Suspension: independent torsion bars front, leaf spring rear.
Tyres: 155SR 13.
Dimensions, length: 3880mm (12ft 8.75in); width: 1537mm (5ft 0.5in); height: 1378mm (4ft 6.25in); wheelbase: 2254mm (7ft 4.75in); weight-unladen: 864 kg (1905 lb).
Capacities, engine sump: 3.31 litres (5.75 Imp. pints); fuel tank: 42 litres (9.25 Imp. gal); cooling system: 4.8 litres (8.5 Imp. pints).
  Notes: Originally Daf 66. Three-door (estate) shown. Two-door (saloon) also available. Latest versions have modifications to interior fittings and seats.

VOLVO (S)

343 DL

1397cc

Chassis: unitary construction.
Engine: front-mounted, four-cylinder, in-line, ohv, water-cooled, bore 76mm, stroke 77mm, output 70 bhp at 5500 rev/min, torque 11 kgf.m (80 lbf.ft) at 3500 rev/min, compression ratio: 9.5:1.
Carburettor: Solex, single.
Clutch: N/A.
Transmission: Continuously variable automatic.
Final Drive: rear wheels.
Brakes: disc front, drum rear, servo-assisted.
Steering: rack and pinion.
Suspension: independent coil spring front, leaf spring rear.
Tyres: 155SR 13.
Dimensions, length: 3683mm (13ft 9in); width: 1664mm (5ft 5.25in); height: 1397mm (4ft 7in); wheelbase: 2349mm (7ft 10.25in); weight-unladen: 978 kg (2154 lb).
Capacities, engine sump: 3.3 litres (5.75 Imp. pints); fuel tank: 45 litres (10 Imp. gal); cooling system: 4.8 litres (8.5 Imp. pints).
   Notes: Introduced 1976. Three-door hatchback incorporating improved DAF variomatic transmission and Renault engine. De Dion rear axle and rear-mounted gearbox/differential.

VOLVO (S)

244 DL   **2127cc**

Chassis: unitary construction.
Engine: front-mounted, four-cylinder, in-line, ohc, water-cooled, bore 92mm, stroke 80mm, output 100 bhp at 5250 rev/min, torque 17.3 kgf.m (125 lbf.ft) at 3000 rev/min, compression ratio: 8.5:1.
Carburettor: Stromberg, single.
Clutch: diaphragm, sdp.
Transmission: 4F1R, manual a/s.
Final Drive: rear wheels.
Brakes: disc front and rear, servo-assisted.
Steering: rack and pinion, power-assisted.
Suspension: independent coil spring front, coil spring rear.
Tyres: 175HR 14.
Dimensions, length: 4898mm (16ft 0.75in); width: 1707mm (5ft 7.25in); height: 1435mm (4ft 8.5in); wheelbase: 2640mm (8ft 8in); weight-unladen: 1383 kg (3047 lb).
Capacities, engine sump: 3.8 litres (6.75 Imp. pints); fuel tank: 60 litres (13.25 Imp. gal); cooling system: 9.5 litres (16.75 Imp. pints).
   Notes: Introduced 1974. Also available is a 244 GL model (123 bhp, fuel injection engine). Estate car versions designated 245DL and 245DLE. Latest models have improved performance and modifications to the seats and windscreen wipers. Externally, the revised grille now encloses the headlights and rear marker lights are fitted.

VOLVO (S)

264 GLE

2664cc

Chassis: unitary construction.
Engine: front-mounted, six-cylinder, v-configuration, ohc, water-cooled, bore 88mm, stroke 73mm, output 140 bhp at 6000 rev/min, torque 20.8 kgf.m (150 lbf.ft) at 3000 rev/min, compression ratio: 8.7:1.
Carburettor: N/A (fuel injection).
Clutch: diaphragm, sdp.
Transmission: 3F1R, automatic.
Final Drive: rear wheels.
Brakes: disc front and rear, servo-assisted.
Steering: rack and pinion, power-assisted.
Suspension: independent coil springs front, coil spring rear.
Tyres: 185/70HR 14.
Dimensions, length: 4898mm (16ft 1in); width: 1707mm (5ft 7.25in); height: 1435mm (4ft 8.5in); wheelbase: 2640mm (8ft 8in); weight-unladen 1475 kg (3245 lb).
Capacities, engine sump: 6.5 litres (11.5 Imp. pints); fuel tank: 60 litres (13.25 Imp. gal); cooling system: 11 litres (19.25 Imp. pints).
   Notes: Introduced 1974. Features Bosch fuel-injection equipment. Also available is the 264 GL with either manual or automatic transmission.

INDEX BY MAKE

INDEX BY MAKE

INDEX BY MAKE

INDEX BY MAKE

INDEX BY MAKE

INDEX BY MAKE

INDEX BY MAKE